CALL of the HEART

*Awakened,
The Journey of Self-Love*

BRIAN ROSCOE

CALL OF THE HEART: AWAKENED, THE JOURNEY OF SELF-LOVE
COPYRIGHT © 2019 BY BRIAN ROSCOE

ALL RIGHTS RESERVED. NO PART OF THIS PUBLICATION MAY BE REPRODUCED, DISTRIBUTED, OR TRANSMITTED IN ANY FORM OR BY ANY MEANS, INCLUDING PHOTOCOPYING, RECORDING, OR OTHER ELECTRONIC OR MECHANICAL METHODS, WITHOUT THE PRIOR WRITTEN PERMISSION OF THE AUTHOR, EXCEPT IN THE CASE OF BRIEF QUOTATIONS EMBODIED IN CRITICAL REVIEWS AND CERTAIN OTHER NONCOMMERCIAL USES PERMITTED BY COPYRIGHT LAW.

THE CONTENT OF THIS BOOK IS FOR GENERAL INFORMATIONAL PURPOSES ONLY. IT IS NOT MEANT TO BE USED, NOR SHOULD IT BE USED, TO DIAGNOSE OR TREAT ANY MEDICAL CONDITION OR TO REPLACE THE SERVICES OF YOUR PHYSICIAN OR OTHER HEALTHCARE PROVIDER. THE ADVICE AND STRATEGIES CONTAINED IN THE BOOK MAY NOT BE SUITABLE FOR ALL READERS.

NEITHER THE AUTHOR, PUBLISHER, NOR ANY OF THEIR EMPLOYEES OR REPRESENTATIVES GUARANTEES THE ACCURACY OF INFORMATION IN THIS BOOK OR ITS USEFULNESS TO A PARTICULAR READER, NOR ARE THEY RESPONSIBLE FOR ANY DAMAGE OR NEGATIVE CONSEQUENCE THAT MAY RESULT FROM ANY TREATMENT, ACTION TAKEN, OR INACTION BY ANY PERSON READING OR FOLLOWING THE INFORMATION IN THIS BOOK.

FOR PERMISSION REQUESTS OR TO CONTACT THE AUTHOR, VISIT:
INSPIRATIONALESPRESSO.ORG

ISBN-13: 9780997647624

PRINTED IN THE UNITED STATES OF AMERICA

CALL of the HEART

Awakened, the journey of self-love

BRIAN ROSCOE

Dedicated to you, the reader,
as you continue on your committed and precious journey
from living in your head to living through your heart.

AWAKENED
Welcome TO YOUR JOURNEY

How vast are the secrets to self-love? Could it even be possible that only six exist? I suspect something inside of you already knows the answer to that. All you need to do is begin exploring some of the authors, philosophers, and inspirational speakers who teach love and you'll see soon enough that the lists made on behalf of self-love are extensive. So the job of listing all the secrets of all the self-love living within and through you is far beyond the context of this book or any other. Needless to say, it would require multiple volumes of writing to even begin to define it all.

In *Call of the Heart,* we attempt to touch on some of the potential ideas of self-love that are important to the human journey and which tend to expand within us as we move through them. The concepts of self-love presented in these books will give you a vital primer for your journey, and they can help you make space within for the rest of love to naturally come forward. These are six obvious secrets of the expressions of love that integrate with one another, and they expand into our lives in many ways and in seemingly infinite directions. As you work with them, there's an

understanding of love that automatically grows within you and helps you work through the bumps of life in a more profound and gentle way—so much so that we often find it impossible to ignore our ability to bring love forward, that living without it is just not possible anymore. Yes, there are many more secrets and truths to this self-love, much more to be known, but, in the context of this book, we've narrowed it down to some core concepts of love. We've done so hoping that this can be a powerful beginning for that sacred journey into your own heart, a rekindling of your deepest personal truths. My sincere hope is that *Call of the Heart* profoundly touches your heart, that love springs forward from you, to you, and through you so that you might brighten this world with a quality of light that is purely yours, which will mean that it is purely good.

My goal in writing is to help people see life from a deeper perspective, through a lens of love—to help them know and befriend a love that expands their hearts, even when love doesn't seem real or very available in this life. I see my work as helping us all with opening up to and remembering our deeper selves, especially in remembering the preciousness of what we were designed to be: a spiritual heart in human form, whether we do it in difficulty, sadness, or joy.

There's a difference between knowing that path and walking the path. Walking the path requires stepping forward into our journey with the great intention of learning love, while understanding there's really no other way back to ourselves except through that love. Learning that we are love is a required step if we truly wish to grow within ourselves, if we honestly want to evolve through our hearts. My goal is to help people see life more clearly from the perspective of the essence of their expanding heart.

This journey is a relentless call to heart. It never gives up on you, and there's absolutely no reason for you to give up on it. There's always space to shift, and at points in life, we all need to be in this world differently than how we have learned so far. Find a little patience within yourself so that the journey has its best and deepest meaning for you. Let it rock your world so you have no choice but to change your quality of thinking, no option but to open your heart. In doing so, it helps you see that your peace is always there to be had, and when you go deeper, you realize it always was.

CONTENTS

Introduction. i

Notes on Gratitude. 1
Remembering Your Spirited Essence. 44
Living Through Love. 80
Honoring the Beautiful Creation of You (*You are Enough*). 134
Tapping into Your Personal Presence. 170
Recognizing the Gifts in the Wound (*The Lessons of Being Human*). . . 224
Expanding Perspectives of the Heart. 264

Conclusion. 316

INTRODUCTION

When the Navajos weave a rug, they intentionally leave little imperfections throughout the tapestry with a purpose. They believe that nothing is perfect except God, and to pretend that it is, is simply unproductive to the spirit of our journey. It's believed that through the imperfections intentionally placed in that piece that the spirit finds the capacity to flow into and through the rug. It seems to be similar with us. Our imperfections allow us to make all the mistakes that we learn about ourselves through the imperfections of the human that God flows through. So when we're trying to be perfect, not only is it unproductive to our lives, it's exhausting to us because, in truth, we're trying to do something that's just not and never was meant to be possible. Trying to live our lives in perfection just becomes pointless and often disruptive noise in the mind, it only depletes us. So be okay with your imperfections. If anything, allow them to rejuvenate you, not deplete you, because, like the Navajo rug, if we see our flaws with grace, that our imperfections are placed in us with purpose, that's where God flows through us, offering potential opportunities for growth.

> *"We are all just walking each other home."*
> –Ram Dass

Only in our thinking can we make ourselves strangers to one another. We're all together on this soulful journey, all together living the adventure of remembering our truth. We're journey friends of a common thread moving through this busy, confusing world of joy, struggle, happiness, and pain. As we step into life with courage and love rather than anxiety and fear, the life experiences we encounter can be greeted with far more grace and strength because we're actively living through our heart. We can move in the world knowing more clearly what our best is, and understand one another in a healthier, more open-minded way. On this journey, we all work hard, struggling in our uniquely human ways, working to eliminate old negative thinking and to do our best to understand the limitations in our thinking.

Life needs us to participate in its adventure, and together, we explore for and remember our humanity, our truth, and, through that, our identity. Our work is to reclaim our sacred place in this beautiful world, to satisfy our yearning for life with one another that reflects the depth of our love. No matter the circumstances, our desire is to touch joy and to live in this world, greeting all beings and entering all rooms heart first.

I hope this book touches you and your journey. I hope it helps propel you into yourself, into your natural, inspired state of being, one alive to your life. I hope that it helps you move forward into your life of remembering your precious heart and seeing the hearts of others as no different from your own. Namasté.

("Namasté" is a Hindu greeting that means "The divine in me bows to the divine in you," reflecting the belief that the divine self is the same in all.)

If I write about anything, it's probably about ways to find hope in the difficult and confusing situations of life, and then to reframe them with greater potentials so that we might approach them with love.

The things I write about give people permission to think, to open up to new ideas, and to further explore ideas they've thought about but didn't have the words to express. My writing might take them a little further down the road to processing a thought they had about their true nature that they didn't previously know what to do with.

My writing always points in the same direction: redirecting the habits of the mind toward peace, expanding our awareness of spirit, and helping to remember love's presence within.

Each of the entries in this book is a meditation in itself. There doesn't need to be an order to the way you go through it, although we have tried to present it in a framework that tries to clarify it and help make the material more available to your journey. As you come across particular passages that you find yourself connecting with, let yourself linger in them as long as you need. Find a part of yourself in them.

AUTHOR'S NOTE

While writing my first book, *Inspirational Espresso*, my ten-year-old daughter, Eliska (Ellie), asked me what it was about. I puffed up a bit and proudly told her I was writing a book to help people find ways to think and live in a gentler way, to remember how to be kinder to one another and create a more peaceful life experience for themselves. And she got it! She paused, and said that she thinks a lot about being kinder to people. I was so impressed! I thought, *That's my girl! From out of the mouths of babes!* Ellie went on to explain, "But it's so hard and, usually, it's just easier to be mean." Ahhh! And we were so close!

Sometimes it's just about recognizing the journey—that alone requires courage. Ellie had the chutzpah to see the journey and recognize its difficulty. There's a strength, a courage we need to acquire on this path, one that requires you to look at what's in front of you, understand when you're stuck, and then internally find the grit to step up to your journey and search for your better way—the way of wisdom, the way of your truth, and the way of the heart.

Journey: *Suggesting travel or passage from one place to another. For example: moving from a place of internal judgment and ill will to forgiveness and release.*

Courage: *Mental or moral strength to venture, persevere, and withstand danger, fear, or difficulty.*

Journey Courage: *The act of supporting the personal strength and perseverance it takes to move forward in our life experience. To step away from who and what we may have become and into who and what we've always been meant to be. It's about you playing the pivotal role in your own personal evolution and life experience.*

NOTES ON GRATITUDE

Ahhh, gratitude, gratitude, gratitude. The often forgotten child of love. The healer of our chattering mind, shifter of our destructive attitudes, and opener of hidden doors within our heart. Gratitude helps us see all parts of our life with a new and great attitude, it uncovers understanding when we're confused, and lightens everything that feels heavy and burdensome in our lives. Gratitude: so easy to be pushed to the side in our busy life and yet essential to the fullness of being alive. Gratitude, gratitude, gratitude, thank you for your patience, your undying trust. I do not wish to neglect you. I will write your name on the back of my hand, tattoo you on my mind. Gratitude, let's get to know each other, let's bond, let's get married right now!

> "I don't have to chase extraordinary moments to find happiness—
> it's right in front of me if I'm paying attention and practicing gratitude."
> -Brené Brown

Grateful for ALL the Gifts

If we're sensitive, we notice that, as we walk past one another, we're subtly aware of imbalances that exist within and between each other. We might walk past someone and feel an air of negativity, instability, sadness, or anger of some nature—feeling somehow disturbed or disrupted by the frequency and tone of the aberrant energy we've just experienced, not necessarily even being fully aware of what happened, but we know we're feeling something within, something disruptive to our internal world. The truth is, that's just us feeling the energy of our environment. There's nothing to be alarmed about or scared of (assuming violence isn't part of the picture). It helps to see it as more of an information gathering moment for us, and it's important to never take those information gathering sessions personally. They're an ongoing experience for all humans. Our job is to simply allow that momentary experience of someone else's struggle to simply be what it is; to do our best to avoid creating toxic thought or drama around it, and to find a place of compassion to view it from while wishing everyone involved well. It's our way of accepting and blessing life as it moves through us.

As we evolve, we give permission to the universe to use us in whatever way is necessary. We give ourselves permission to become purifiers for the world, to help one another deal with and heal from the effects of the energy generated in the world around us. It helps to remember that we were never promised a pain-free trip, we were just promised growth. Sometimes our greatest gratitude is derived through the trials we've endured to become who we are. **Be grateful for the gifts within**

the wound. It's a kindness to ourselves, and it opens up a direct path to knowing, in a very real way, to the core of compassion and forgiveness and how it works through us.

> *"Gratitude is the healthiest of all human emotions. The more you express gratitude for what you have, the more likely you will have even more to express gratitude for."*
> *-Zig Ziglar*

If our ultimate goal is to find a kindness with one another, what better avenue could there be than gratitude and forgiveness?

> *"When I started counting my blessings, my whole life turned around."*
> *-Willie Nelson*

The heart of gratitude is based in our love for this life.

"It is impossible to feel grateful and depressed in the same moment."
-Naomi Williams

When we're stuck in any kind of negative thinking, gratitude offers us a place to rest and heal. Gratitude helps us return to that quality of precious thought that we all yearn for, thinking that most reflects our truth because it starts from a feeling in the heart. It's not a reflection from the mind. It's reflected to the mind as it moves from the heart upward into our thinking. Gratitude's initial spark comes from a pure place within, it gives the mind the opportunity to begin again, presenting a chance to open to thoughts that heal rather than feeding the thinking that disrupts us. Gratitude adds grace to our thinking and our lives and awakens our heart to the moment in front of us right now.

"The roots of all goodness lie in the soil of appreciation for goodness."
-Dalai Lama

Unlived desires, unrealized expectations: like most things in life, they're either greeted by a compassion, an understanding and a gratitude for life, for who we are, who we've become and what we have now, or by the yearning and lament for what we feel we've lost or never received. These are two diametrically opposing responses that impact the human spirit. One depletes life and is a form of self limiting thought, the other opens us up to new possibilities and frees us to move forward. Both are choices.

Exercise:
Take a minute to define this for yourself, to answer this question:

What depletes your ability to have gratitude for life?

What cultivates gratitude in you, breathes life into it?

"There are only two ways to live your life. One is as though nothing is a miracle. The other is as though everything is a miracle."
-Albert Einstein

Regret has screwed with my life for fifty-six years, and damnit, I'm finally ready to change that!

My goal is to find gratitude for what I am and all I have despite any of life's disappointments, to release myself from past regrets wherever and whenever they pop up, and to be alive and present to where I am right now! My goal is to appreciate whatever moment I find myself in and see this world, my world, as a gift; to consciously sit in deep gratitude of this precious, one-of-a-kind, singular chance to appreciate the gift—a gift meant to open and teach the heart lessons that we can only learn here, as a spirit placed on Earth and tethered to the body of a human being. My goal is to appreciate all that in as many moments as I can.

"People with a scarcity mentality tend to see everything in terms of win-lose. There is only so much; and if someone else has it, that means there will be less for me. The more principle-centered we become, the more we develop an abundance mentality, the more we are genuinely happy for the successes, wellbeing, achievements, recognition, and good fortune of other people. We believe their success adds to rather than detracts from our lives."
-Stephen R. Covey

"Reflect upon your present blessings, of which every man has plenty; not on your past misfortunes, of which all men have some."
-Charles Dickens

Life is inherently driven by love, and everything good, bad or otherwise is initially derived through that love. It's our distortions and disconnect from this truth that encourage ill will within us. But ill will is impossible through the embrace of love.

> *"None is more impoverished than the one who has no gratitude. Gratitude is a currency that we can mint for ourselves, and spend without fear of bankruptcy."*
> -Fred De Witt Van Amburgh

There's a freedom derived through life, embracing it, being present to the moment in front of us right now. We just have to grab our opportunity, open to life and its lessons. Those lessons are the gold, they hold our wisdom and our freedom.

Lauren, my oldest daughter, the one that, by myself, I helped deliver. The midwives didn't make it on time, so with angels surrounding us, we bonded as she took her first breath. Yes, that Lauren. She moved away from everyone and everything she knew in Grand Haven, Michigan several years back so she could find herself! Now, I have to say, I thought she should have stayed here, finished up college. But her plans, very plainly, were otherwise. Something spoke to her in Flagstaff, Arizona, and that's where she is as I write this. But Lauren had to leave, I knew that. Something inside her had to go, explore, detach enough from Grand Haven and her parents, grandparents, and everybody that she previously connected with so that she could remember what's most important. She needed to find and remember the deepest part of who she is, remember the heart of Lauren. And that's a process without end, for all of us. When we listen to that whisper, there's no telling where we might end up—in school, out of school, in a great job, wonderful relationship, living in an exciting area of the world we'd never heard of before, or away from all that, immersed in situations we need to struggle through. Our life takes on a design that's quite unexpected when we follow the journey of the heart. And so, for Lauren, it took her to Flagstaff, Arizona.

> "Each one of us just wants to be noticed and loved and accepted exactly as is—not changed or made different."
> -Louise Hay

Leaving to find Lauren. Now that was Lauren's gift to herself, but it was also her gift to me. It forced me to finally get to the place where I simply had to say, "I have no control over this anymore, I have no say in what you do, I have no say in your life and how you live it, whether you live or die is not up to me anymore. Thank you, I love you, and now we are both a little more free." Lauren's leaving impacted me. It took a long time to understand it, but it impacted me and forced me to release any sense of control or responsibility about her life. In her choosing freedom for herself, her strength filtered into my life as well. I can now step back and be her father on a higher level, be her friend and confidant, and just allow her the space to live her life. There's a sadness and a joy in that knowledge, but more than anything, there's growth. And a reclaiming of the self, for both of us.

My most wonderful daughter, Lauren, your life is now and forever will be whatever you want it to be, and it's going to follow the path that you choose. The choices that we make determine the lives that we live. Whatever life becomes or doesn't become, you need to address. It's not about me, your friends, the president, or your religious conviction, because, in the end, you make all the choices, and within that, you drive your life's trajectory.

It's true in everything—divorce, new relationships, jobs—we're responsible for ourselves. That's it. The way we choose to think, the choices we make, will absolutely determine the quality and tone of the lives that we live. And it's inevitably up to us. Only we can make those choices—what to think and how to proceed. I wish you well in your thoughts and your deeds.

*"Some people grumble that roses have thorns;
I am grateful that thorns have roses."
-Alphonse Karr*

Deb

Deb, one of my oldest and most dear friends, called me one Sunday very excited about an experience she'd had. She had experienced her own perfect moment of inspiration, which she humorously referred to as, "My evangelical me."

On a sleepless night, she had been struggling with the imminent death of a friend. She found herself asking what she was bringing into the world and leaving behind. Asking herself what the "legacy of Deb" looked like. And in her quiet moment of awakened early morning darkness, she had an authentically personal thought and experience that held her mind and heart tightly. It was a moment of epiphany that was hers alone to be with in that early morning hour. Deb's inspiration had come through her heart, becoming the words that would inspire her to stay on point in her world, to keep walking with a deep breath of aliveness to her life. It was her way of attaching to love's presence. Deb's phrase was "Spread kindness and joy to everyone you meet and give thanks for every day." This was her power statement, meant for her, and true for everyone. It came through her to spark the very soul of who she is.

"Spread kindness and joy to everyone you meet and give thanks for every day" is the statement that puts Deb back on track when she's feeling struggle, attack, and vulnerability. It's what she remembers when she's immersed in gratitude for what she's been given in this life. It's the statement that touches her heart on a moment-to-moment basis, inspiring her toward a quality of life that keeps her grounded and in a state

of tenderness and joy. This is Deb's personal definition of love. It's her reminder of who she is.

Statements like this can come through and belong to any of us. We'll choose different words depending on who we are, but it's the essence of the words, the message behind them, that will draw us in toward our heart. Their message will always have a common underlying theme. Remember love, remember your truth. It's how those words speak to our heart and the feelings that they cultivate within us that truly build a picture for us to live by. So now, find that perfect statement that works for you, that inspires you toward your love. Use Deb's if you want, or just explore until the words of your heart unfold for you.

"'Enough' is a feast."
-Buddhist proverb

LAYERS OF GRATITUDE

The layers of gratitude are expansive. We can find gratitude in whatever experience we encounter in our lives. The only requirement is keeping your eyes open to all the possibilities for it to be experienced in this radical life of ours. We naturally find little gratitudes to feel when we enjoy a special food, drink, or personal activity; tiny pleasures when we're petting a dog, talking to an old friend, or using our new ice maker—the one we've been wanting for years while preparing a meal. These grateful attitudes can spring forward at any moment as we see life with a smile of appreciation. I call these grata-bites, tiny little bite-sized moments of gratitude that are easy to swallow and nurturing for the body.

Little gratitude: the appreciation of the moments of our life, the spontaneous moments of recognition that we have been given a beautiful life. Grata-bites often inspire almost a subconscious moment of breath and a smile. We really like to share these with one another.

And then there's big gratitude! The "I see God" gratitude! The gratitude acknowledging our inspired presence to the world! The grat-

itude that takes you straight out of your body! Grata-Kong gratitude! Here, you have to stop whatever you're doing because life as you know it shifts. You feel like you can't possibly hold the entirety of what you're experiencing. Suddenly, what you thought was real changes, and the only real thing to you is love and the presence of that miracle in your life. It's a pure masterpiece of inspiration. When you're in Grata-Kong, everyone needs to just leave you alone and let you be in your feelings. It's a show-stopping, prayerful time in which your breath is literally taken away.

Look at all the layers of gratitude as you experience them in your life. Add to this list. You know you're in gratitude when:

- you're sitting in awe, quietly watching something of the world: a baby, children playing, the earth moving around you in some new, previously unseen way, a cloud formed, a sunrise or sunset that catches your breath, a close look at the complexity of an insect, a molecule, a picture of space…

- you find yourself remembering all that your life has inspired in those around you, realized some small purpose of your life as it relates to others…

- you see and realize the many ways your life has been graced, beyond any difficulty and drama, and often the difficulties can even be seen as critical players in your moments of grace…

- you're laughing or crying with a joy that emanates through

your very being…

- you're giving freely of yourself without expecting anything in return, receiving only the beauty of your own giving…

- you're able to take joy in the success of others…

- you stop dead in your tracks and stare at the world with awe…

- you realize you know a deep, inspired love, and you feel it as it flows through you…

- you find a state of gratitude every time you find a quote that touches you. I, personally, feel grateful that others have been inspired to write them down and share their hearts with the world. I'm struck by the fact of how many of us are working toward the same direction in life, trying to define our deepest understanding of life, to learn the lessons of what it is to be human in this world and surround it with a strength that allows us to know our own hearts…

- you stop for a moment to appreciate a song, a piece of art, the patterns of a floor tile, the grain in a piece of wood, the frozen patterns in a piece of ice…

All of these represent but a tiny portion, a speck, of the many levels of gratitude we can embrace in life.

Essentially, we are blessed with gratitude every time we allow ourselves to be alive to the beauty and awake to the truth that lays behind all of our lives, and present within the gift of living, the gifts already placed in our heart. Gratitude is always, in some way, attached to all that life has to offer, sometimes blatant, often so subtle that they're easily missed. If you want to know gratitude, you need coffee, you have to stay awake to its presence, feel it, and it will come. Gratitude is always there for the taking; it's always there to help us heal our lives.

"He who plants kindness gathers love."
-Saint Basil, the Great (329-379), Bishop of Cesarea

"If you count all your assets, you always show a profit."
-Robert Quillen

Often, the intensity of a challenge roughly relates to the depth and quality of the lesson derived through that challenge.

The universe just wants you to grow, and it doesn't mind compromising your happiness for the moment, giving you a bit of pain and struggle to spark up its lesson, to make sure you know growth is on the table. Sometimes we need an attention grabber, even a stinging slap, and the universe is more than happy to supply. Without the human struggle and drama we encounter in life, we wouldn't have a framework to receive our lessons through. Without that, we would never have the same opportunity to receive the gifts we do. Our lessons have a tendency of coordinating with the intensity of our struggles. It's difficult, but that's what creates a framework for us to grow through. As irrational or contrary to our best interest as that might feel, there's a very real truth to it. Be grateful for your trials. They build character and an ability to grow and move forward in this life. They help you find your strength, and cultivate a sharable compassion, understanding, and ability to love. And that's just unattainable through a life of pure ease.

"Acknowledging the good that you already have in your life is the foundation for all abundance."
-Eckhart Tolle

The recognition of any disconnect, any distraction from who we are, the disruption of our truth or wellbeing at any level, is a gift. It's our minds way of saying, "I found something that's not quite working to our benefit, not helping us stay on the old peace train!" It's a natural part of being human that we catch ourselves in this kind of off-centered glitch. In a quiet moment, it's easy to see that within that "lucky catch" lays the miracle of thought and consciousness. In a very real way, it's us participating in life as it flows through us.

After the recognition, the next step, the action to be taken, or the next thought, is in our field. It's our responsibility to move forward from recognizing where we're stuck. And you can either do something with it, or you stay the same. That's pretty much the choice, take it or... take it!

So you ask, *Where's the gratitude in this?* **Well**, our potential for gratitude lays in having the ability to recognize when we're off track, the grace to self-correct, and having enough self-love to care.

To have that ability to love yourself, to care enough about who you're becoming and to have developed a strength of character that wants to do something about it, well, that's a miracle—a musical of life worth being grateful for, grateful to have, the privilege to participate in this world, in this precious human form. For this, despite the difficulty, we can have gratitude.

"You may encounter many defeats, but you must not be defeated. In fact, it may be necessary to encounter the defeats, so you can know who you are, what you can rise from, how you can still come out of it."
-Maya Angelou

"Gratitude turns what we have into enough, and more. It turns denial into acceptance, chaos into order, confusion into clarity... it makes sense of our past, brings peace for today, and creates a vision for tomorrow."
-Melody Beattie

Putting on the Worst-Case-Scenario Lens!

Sometimes I have a hard time getting into a space were gratitude can weave its way into my thinking. I know it's happening because I catch myself feeling and usually acting stupid-grouchy with little reason. When I see it, I'll step back and try a grateful attitude reboot. Depending on what's stuck in my head in the moment, I might use the worst-case-scenario lens to look at life. I consider the topic I think has me in a bad mood, and then I look at all the ways it could exist in my life—all the things that could have happened that are less desirable than what I'm dealing with in the moment. I look at all that could have gone wrong or been born wrong in that scenario, and it helps me step back and put things in a better perspective so I can appreciate what I have now. It helps me walk forward from a place of gratitude. That may or may not play a role in how things change, but it sure plays a role in how I change. It allows me to see even the things I don't care for with more grace, see my life as "just right," like Goldilock's porridge.

For example, I might not like the house I live in, but I look at a worst-case-scenario. I look for a scenario that allows me to see all that I have, make space to appreciate where I am in the moment. *I've lost my house in a fire, or it went back to the bank, or I live in a war-torn country…* need I say more?

Using the worst-case-scenario technique when we encounter difficult life experiences helps us find gratitude for all the other possibilities life presents us and an appreciation for what it has spared us from.

Considering the worst case scenario helps you step back from your dance with impending doom and lets you know you're going to be okay, you can handle life, you just need to get okay with being okay—to be where we are, happy for the opportunity to be alive, trusting our process, and feeling enough, lovable, and loved. Like most of our lessons, knowing gratitude is more about being immersed in moving in its direction, learning more and more about how it impacts our lives, not necessarily arriving at some final destination.

"The world has enough beautiful mountains and meadows, spectacular skies and serene lakes. It has enough lush forests, flowered fields, and sandy beaches. It has plenty of stars and the promise of a new sunrise and sunset every day. What the world needs more of is people to appreciate and enjoy it."
-Michael Josephson

When we come to the realization that some of the attitudes that we hold as true, perhaps even set in stone, ideas that we may have thought were important but on examination seem to be holding us back from exploring ourselves, from knowing our truth, it allows us to see two directions in our life more clearly:

A. We can step back and observe the world we used to live in, our past beliefs, the old thinking we previously called home. It's a place we inhabited, that, for a time, may have been useful to us, but now has become inefficient, obsolete and irrelevant in our world today.

B. We get a deeper sense, a vision, of where we might go, who we might become. We see the directions yet to be fully explored, and although different and scary, we recognize that they're exciting and alive to us as well. We get a glimpse into a new, more fulfilling way to think, and within that, if we choose, to live.

*"Gratitude is a currency that we can mint for ourselves,
and spend without fear of bankruptcy."
-Fred de Witt Van Amburgh*

Gratitude's one of the big kahunas on this journey—a quality of being definitely worth striving for. It's one of the major intersections on that big highway of love, and it helps all other qualities of love come alive and unite in a stronger way within us. It's like the crazy glue of the heart! Gratitude helps us put a better, more robust spin on everything we truly desire on this journey, it brightens all the goals of the heart. Whatever we touch in life with gratitude as our partner has a strength attached that did not formally exist. Gratitude builds in a strength of heart to all circumstances and ideas of life.

We have to get down and dirty with gratitude, explore the qualities of what it is to open to it and own its presence in us. We need to ask the big defining questions of the heart: So what does this internal state of gratitude look like? Can we put our thoughts and feelings into words, explaining its presence in our hearts and what influence it has over our lives? What does it look like in our minds, feel like in our hearts, and who do we become when gratitude shines through us? How do we see and relate to others? How do we see ourselves? What becomes of our self-talk and struggle? What new ways of being are created within us, ideas of living with more truth, when we are awake to the gift of gratitude? Who do we become when we employ the gratitude that naturally flows through us, when we uncover the emotional shrouds and distracting ideas that keep us so sleepy to this gift of being?

There are folks out there telling you to have gratitude, explaining what having gratitude does for you, all the biblical and religious teachings that point you in gratitude's direction. But how about when you're not in a state of gratitude? How do you get there? Where are your gratitude

training wheels? What do you do to attain that which you most desire? How do you find that spark when you're stuck in a life that sometimes seems nothing short of difficult and disastrous?

There's information out there about gratitude, but what it is to actually have and live in gratitude? That's a whole other story to explore. Explaining it is like explaining life itself—when we try to explain life's fullness, we come to the conclusion that the bigness of it is, indeed, ineffable. There are no words, it's so deep that it has to exist free of words and held as a heartfelt feeling, a spark of light.

People, however, study and try to expound on gratitude and its benefits. They've found that the benefits people derive from living with deep unbinding gratitude for life are evident in the enhanced quality of our personal relationships, the tendency to better maintain the physical healthcare we're worthy of, enhanced psychological health, emotional balance, maintaining a quality of exercise we enjoy and our bodies respond well to, getting the quality of sleep we need, deeper feelings of self-worth and belonging, and a stronger intellect and mental acuity as we participate in life. You can read about it in a book, but you really can't feel it from those pages. You need to take the journey of owning and preciously embodying it. Being in gratitude requires your emersion in life. It requires you to see life beyond the explainable. It requires you to breathe into the ineffable miracle of all that surrounds you. It's a feel-it-first opportunity, and then, perhaps, try-to-explain-it kind of thing. This is because it initiates from and through your heart first, well before it ever hits your head.

Gratitude finds its origins in the heart, it begins in the heart and quickly flows into the ideas of the mind. So when we are presented with the word "gratitude," we often just smile. We don't even know why, we don't necessarily need an idea. We're just grateful for life, and gratitude has already been planted within us, we just need to access it.

> *"The way to develop the best that is in a person*
> *is by appreciation and encouragement."*
> *–Charles Schwab*

Everything in our lives is temporary. All dramas, thoughts, feelings, personalized troubles of any kind—they're all temporary. Unless, of course, we decide to hold onto something longer than that, turn it into a marathon. However, no matter how long we choose to hold it, that's also temporary, because, after all, we're kind of temporary, too. It's probably easier spending your time in gratitude for what is rather than attaching your life flow to what was.

> "He is a wise man who does not grieve for the things which he has not, but rejoices for those which he has."
> -Epictetus

Age often comes with its gifts and its wisdom, its given insights that us youngins just tend to overlook.

Anna is an older patient in the practice, about eighty-seven years old. She's in great shape, one of those people who never seems to mentally age. One morning before a treatment, she sat down on the table, looked me in the eye, and said with conviction, *"Doc, you know, there's a lot of healing in gratitude, it just seems to relate to everything around me. If I throw some gratitude at it, it heals. It's really quite amazing."*

Well, that was enough for me to pay attention, it inspired me to start exploring gratitude more for myself. Anna was right. Gratitude is quite amazing, and what would we be with the absence of gratitude in our lives? How would we open the doors of our heart? What healing would we have to give up without gratitude in our human toolbox? Could we heal or could we even exist without gratitude in our world? Personally, I don't think so.

"Let us rise up and be thankful, for if we didn't learn a lot today, at least we learned a little, and if we didn't learn a little, at least we didn't get sick, and if we got sick, at least we didn't die; so, let us all be thankful."
-Buddha

Spend some time exploring the ideas and research around this gratitude phenomenon:

- First, look at the teachings that encourage gratitude in us as individuals and society as a whole.

- Second, what's the research out there that supports how gratitude benefits us physically, emotionally, spiritually, and as a culture?

- Third, and perhaps most important, how do we transition ourselves from a life without gratitude to the ability to embrace it? Life that's, perhaps, shrouded in negativity and even a victim mentality to a life that allows us to immerse ourselves in gratitude, that allows us to find a personal definition for gratitude and how it impacts our lives, and embrace a state of being that allows gratitude in and encourages it and recognizes it in as many ways as we're able. How do we transition into a life that reboots the very framework of life as we know it and welcomes gratitude where it was previously unknown or unwelcome.

If you really want something, research it, understand it, do your best to own it.

Gratitude Questions:
- How does gratitude support me?
- How does the lack of gratitude affect me?

- What does that do?
- How does it feel?
- Who do I become?

Gratitude. I don't know if gratitude on its own actually does anything. It needs us. Unless we put it into action, it just sits there, staring at us like a hungry dog, wagging its tail, waiting for recognition. But gratitude is a natural expression of our true nature—it seems to want to be a part of what we're meant to be, to contribute to the quality of being we're asked to explore and embody. To the best of my knowledge, there aren't many teachings out there telling us to avoid gratitude at any cost! So, I think we can safely assume gratitude has a little something going for it. It seems then, we're left with the option to embrace gratitude if we choose, and allow its benefits to spill forward into our lives.

With gratitude in our pocket, suddenly, we're able to appreciate more of life, to explore how love can unfold into everything we think and do. Gratitude is one with love, one with forgiveness, and over time, it naturally gets recognized for its value as we evolve more and more into ourselves, into and through our hearts. Through this, we find our truth as beings of light, beings that just happen to have bodies, apparently just to complicate things, but nevertheless beings that can know love.

> *"Piglet noticed that even though he had a very small heart, it could hold a rather large amount of gratitude."*
> *-A.A. Milne*

Cultivating gratitude requires a very real dedication to ourselves, a bit of practice, and the willingness to expand beyond what we think we can feel, some self-belief and a knowing that we play the ultimate role in determining the quality of our life experience, owning the purity of self-love, understanding that love is all powerful and its essence allows us to stretch beyond any of our fears. Gratitude requires us to acknowledge that the internal quality of our existence is profound evidence that we are love and loved. It's the last part, knowing that we are loved, that needs to be embraced internally. Knowing that we're loved is a big feat, one that we have to find our own, very individual way of seeing. It's true for all of us. It's just that not all of us can necessarily see it that easily. This is perhaps due to the religious dogma we've acquired, or the current state of our life situation, or just a tendency not to trust the world or ourselves. But it doesn't require a religion, and it doesn't require a belief system to know we're emerged in a love that requires nothing but our recognition. It simply requires an opening up to our truth. It's a kind of rationalization we find inside ourselves, simply because we are here, in this miracle, given a body and mind, freedom to determine our thinking, regardless of our circumstances, a freedom that's impossible to remove from our essence. This is love, this is the gift, even though parts of our experience might suck. Therefore, we accept this gift as one of love. Our situations won't always be ideal, but our presence in this world is, and all we ever have for real is the love that we recognize within and help bring forward through connection to our heart.

> "Forget yesterday—it has already forgotten you.
> Don't sweat tomorrow—you haven't even met. Instead, open
> your eyes and your heart to a truly precious gift—today."
> -Steve Maraboli

At some point, while writing *Inspirational Espresso*, it occurred to me how huge this love concept was for us to take into our world. To help myself grasp the vastness of this love, I found myself developing a concept I called "The Holon of Love." It was based in the idea that love, like the universe, is made up of infinite parts—the biggest parts of love, we're aware of, and the tiniest ones, probably not. But the particles all reflect the exact same reflection as the whole. When we separate one part, such as kindness, generosity, forgiveness, compassion, understanding, gratitude, they all have within them the essence of the other. They all reflect every other part of love's presence in the whole. In essence, they are not only part of love, they are, indeed, the whole of love.

If you can't find the wherewithal to be grateful, practice other forms of love and they will naturally lead you toward gratitude over time.

The idea of holon is best described as something that is simultaneously a whole and a part, simultaneously a whole in itself and, at the same time, is nested within another holon, making it a part of something much larger than itself. Thus, the holon of love suggests that all branches of love are simultaneously a part of love and reflect the whole of love. The parts of love cannot exist outside of the presence of the others, and naturally come together to make up something much larger than themselves. The word "love" is the most commonly used word for this phenomena of being, however, even love ceases to exist without the presence of its congruent parts. Without compassion, understanding and kindness, love is not. The same is conversely true for all qualities of love. Love is given to us as a larger than life itself gift to embrace on this human journey of ours.

No matter what quality of love you practice, when it's done with a pure heart, it will bring you closer to gratitude. That's the nature of love. It builds on itself, no matter what the form. It's a holon.

Gratitude naturally exists in all other forms of love.

"In ordinary life, we hardly realize that we receive a great deal more than we give, and that it is only with gratitude that life becomes rich."
-Dietrich Bonhoeffer

Love is a gift to all humans. Everyone has it available to them at any point in their lives. The only trick is, we have to choose it. Love covers all the bases, everything! All events, predicaments, struggles, joys can be integrated with love. If you're having a hard time connecting with gratitude, touch another part of love, explore that, spend some time there and it allows gratitude to evolve, it helps it come out of its shell. Then try exploring it again.

"I truly believe we can either see the connections, celebrate them, and express gratitude for our blessings, or we can see life as a string of coincidences that have no meaning or connection. For me, I'm going to believe in miracles, celebrate life, rejoice in the views of eternity, and hope my choices will create a positive ripple effect in the lives of others. This is my choice."
-Mike Ericksen

Gratitude, Grrrratitude, Gratiduuuude, I'm a Grateful Dude!

Sometimes just saying the word out loud establishes a kind of permission to grow towards it, it gives you the thumbs up to attend your own gratitude party! So, say it. Hear it. Allow gratitude to grow, to become something alive inside of you.

> "Gratitude also opens your eyes to the limitless potential
> of the universe, while dissatisfaction closes your eyes to it."
> -Stephen Richards

Gratitude is one of the keys that we can use to help us live with an open heart. It's surprisingly simple, complete in its function, and when we apply it to our world, it rejuvenates everything that we were ever meant to be. Gratitude relentlessly reminds us that we are love. But the application of gratitude requires our intention to move into it. That's our part. We need to willingly participate in gratitude in order to find the strength of it within and feel the benefits of its presence.

> "Gratitude and attitude are not challenges. They are choices."
> -Robert Braathe

It's impossible to feel negative feelings when gratitude has a hold of you. Gratitude can only birth other positive feelings, it's a holon, a contributor to the whole of life and all the feelings of compassion, kindness, joy, hope, forgiveness, and thanks, which are but a few of the words we use to define the particles that make up this thing we call love.

In the light of gratitude, fear, anguish, anger and negative thinking of all kinds find their potential to be healed. Gratitude brings with it the potential to melt away any of our lingering connections to the suffering we find in life.

> *"This a wonderful day. I've never seen this one before."*
> *-Maya Angelou*

Exercise:
Ask yourself: how does gratitude manifest itself in my life?

Are you able to surround even the difficult situations with understanding and gratitude for the deeper purpose that those moments bring to your life? Are you grateful for the lessons associated with your life—the good, the bad, or the ugly?

What we all bring to one another on the stage of life is perhaps perfectly what it should be, exactly what it's meant to be. It's up to us to work at it, to find its gift.

Can we be grateful to all the people who have participated in our life? Participated at levels nobody understood? These are the people who sacrificed themselves, and we sacrificed ourselves for them. Can we be grateful for their joining us in the journey?

I'm grateful that we have been part of each other's journey. What a beautiful opportunity it has been, thank you. I wish you health, strength and happiness, and all of the beauty life can offer.

"They both seemed to understand that describing it was beyond their powers, the gratitude that spreads through your body when a burden gets lifted, and the sense of homecoming that follows, when you suddenly remember what it feels like to be yourself."
-Tom Perrotta

"The invariable mark of wisdom is to see the miraculous in the common."
-Ralph Waldo Emerson

"In life, one has a choice to take one of two paths: to wait for some special day, or to celebrate each special day."
-Rasheed Ogunlaru

"Suppose two astronauts go to the moon. When they arrive, they have an accident and find out that they have only enough oxygen for two days. There is no hope of someone coming from Earth in time to rescue them. They have only two days to live. If you asked them at that moment, 'What is your deepest wish?' they would answer, 'To be back home, walking on the beautiful planet Earth.' That would be enough for them; they would not want anything else. They would not want to be the head of a large corporation, a big celebrity or president of the United States. They would not want anything except to be back on Earth, to be walking on Earth, enjoying every step, listening to the sounds of nature and holding the hand of their beloved while contemplating the moon.

We should live every day like people who have just been rescued from the moon. We are on Earth now, and we need to enjoy walking on this precious beautiful planet. The Zen master Lin Chi said, 'The miracle is not to walk on water but to walk on the Earth.' I cherish that teaching. I enjoy just walking, even in busy places, like airports and railway stations. In walking like that, with each step caressing our Mother Earth, we can inspire other people to do the same. We can enjoy every minute of our lives."

-Thich Nhat Hanh

As life goes on, I don't think it necessarily gets easier. You become stronger in some ways, smarter in other ways. Hopefully you know yourself better, but I don't think easier is always part of the equation, it just moves and grows, becoming, in many ways, different. Life comes with its undelivered expectations, unfulfilled hopes and desires, and disappointments. No matter who you are, you will not have everything that you believe you want. We will have desires in life that will have to be left behind. So find gratitude for what you have now, because lamenting on what you don't have, crying about what's not even real, accomplishes nothing! It just imprisons the heart.

Being okay with what is requires us to trust life, to trust that everything is just as it needs to be. Yes, life comes with its unfulfilled expectations. But love trusts in the process of us, and connecting with gratitude for all that we have takes the sting out of what you think you've been denied.

> "So much has been given to me; I have no time to ponder
> over that which has been denied."
> -Helen Keller

Without choosing a good human maintenance program, our life experience becomes rather muted and incomplete. Our bodies have been created to act as a receiver for our human experience. It's a filter for the transmission of this universal energy we call inspiration. It's meant to flow into and through us, and it's our responsibility to maintain our emotional-biological machine. We need to pay attention to the quality of physical and emotional fuel we feed ourselves, fortify our lives with. We are responsible for the care and maintenance of the environment that we live in. It's our payment due for the privilege of living life as people!

A Little Better: Take One Great Big ¼ Step… Forward?

Appreciate and have gratitude for all your personal improvement, no matter what it is, the smallest progress in your journey, even when things seem only "a little better." A little better is good. It has a way of unfolding beyond itself, multiplying as you hold it. Over time, a little better can accumulate into "Yeah, this is definitely better." So celebrate that quarter-step forward rather than sitting in the expectation that everything needs to be done now, and perfectly. Perfect is overrated, and it's impossible anyway; we can never reach perfection in this environment, nor are we meant to. We are, however, meant to continuously work at doing our best over and over again, with the objective being to spiral upward toward greater understanding of who we are, how we want to live our lives, and knowing our truth. That is our "perfect."

JOURNEY PROMPT

Gratitude, gratitude, gratitude. Our healing finds its momentum through the gratitude we hold for our lives.

Do a little exercise for yourself:

Consider a struggle, make it one off of your top five list of life struggles. Now, pay attention to how it might have felt to not bring any gratitude into it, nothing but negativity and ill will surrounding it. And then take a look at that same struggle unfolding into your life, explore it, but this time, you're able to surround it with gratitude, see that your life is precious, regardless of the obstacles that naturally occur. Pay attention to what each scenario feels like. Each one is going to have a certain resonance in your heart, pay attention to that feeling. Now ask yourself: where and how would you rather live?

When we forget gratitude, we forget who we are.

JOURNEY PROMPT

This statement, "When we forget gratitude, we forget who we are," is such a mouthful to our soul. Because putting gratitude to the side, we also forget love and kindness, and the only other direction to go is inevitably fear-based—pretty much the opposite direction of love. In that, nothing looks pure, gentle, or beautiful. In fear, our world just doesn't look as good as when we view it through love and gratitude. When we're in a state of mind where gratitude and love just don't seem available to us, the road gets lonely, self-destructive, and we live in the denial of our heart's truth. We forget what it is to embrace our life with acceptance and joy, and we simply forget to see our miracle.

How many times do you find yourself stuck in negative thinking that's simply the result of not being grateful for the life you have? Well, step yourself back. Understand that life wasn't meant to be perfect, and try to touch a little bit of gratitude anyway. Stretch yourself, try to find a way to love what's in front of you on this journey of becoming love. That doesn't mean you have to like everything. Love doesn't require that! You're only asked to have gratitude for living, despite the warbles in your life. And if you do find yourself stuck in negativity, well, remember, nothing is more healing to our hearts than gratitude.

Life is continuously unfolding for us in all ways. There's a skill to observing and stepping over the cracks, an art to appreciating the flowers and the weeds as they appear on our path.

JOURNEY PROMPT

There is so much medicine in gratitude. Gratitude swells our heart, cultivates our strength. It's gratitude which adds a sparkle that helps you to see all life as a gift regardless of the flavor of the moment. Our journey may not require gratitude, but it's gratitude that sparks a brightness into it, and gratitude that helps us know just how vibrantly alive we already are. Would you really want to live without it?

REMEMBERING YOUR
spirited ESSENCE

*"I took a deep breath and listened to that old bray of my heart:
I am, I am, I am."*
-Sylvia Plath

We're all here in this world for the same reason, to claim our inheritance. And you ask, *What is that "inheritance" we're supposed to be claiming? Because I sure could use a bigger house or a new car!* But our inheritance is more than any of that, more than anything material. Our inheritance was placed in the center of our hearts, placed there in a timeless moment to reflect back to us our essence of love when we ask for it. It's our reclaiming of what we are meant to be.

*"Reclaim your belonging, first by reconnecting with your soul,
and then by loving your world from that powerful inner center
of love, sovereignty and wholeness."*
-Hiro Boga

How would we know who we were if the question was not asked, the doubt not sparked within us as to who we are and who we are not?

We're all meant to embrace a uniqueness of our own choosing, to love ourselves and one another despite our lack of understanding. What could be more honoring to God than accepting the differences we all share, exploring together our own distinctive character, and celebrating one another's courage to be oneself? All we have to do is get our heads out of the picture and embrace one another with our hearts. Yay, hearts!

Allow what moves through you with light to speak,
then listen… simply listen.

There's purpose behind everything, with reasons that are beyond what we can know. It requires us to open to a grace brought into our lives only through knowing trust. We must learn the power of trust.

> **Trust.** It's a big word,
> and you spend a lifetime trying to figure it out.

Trust yourself, trust that the unknown in you yet has purpose. We grow into ourselves, rediscover all the truth that exists within us, we learn the love that we are, and we expand into the world with the light that shines from within us. How can we be anything but struck with awe by what we are? How can we feel anything but love for ourselves? How can we see anything around us but the pure abundance of this miracle? Ask yourself: are we not blessed with life, and are we not made of love?

*"We have two lives, and the second begins
when we realize we only have one."*
-Confucius

When you hear a whisper, notice that spark of the mind that says, "There's more light to be shined through you than you know—there's a deeper journey to be lived," and it opens unnoticed doors within that you can never close again. Your heightened awareness makes it impossible to continue in the world as you have. You have no choice, you must walk differently, you must evolve and survive. And so, you live your life beyond what you previously believed yourself to be, because you have chosen to grow, and you have chosen the path of being alive to your life.

The goal of enlightenment is to be present to your journey, to open to the agelessness of your being before you mistakenly get caught up in believing that you can get old. It's about lightening up before your lights turn out, letting go of your rigidity before your rigor mortis sets in. It's learning to live your life before life chooses differently for you, and letting go of our ideas of what life "should be" so that we can just be what we're meant to be.

All of this requires the will to step beyond our thinking, to go beyond our beliefs about what we need to become, and to return to the heart of this life. To be present to our miracle, present to the gift, present to ourselves. After all, they're all the same.

Because life, being in this world, is not about being in control, it never was. That's an illusion created by a fearful, disconnected mind. It's about being okay with what is and living your life, being one with your love despite the fact that the world strives to convince you otherwise. It's the knowing that control is an elusive fox that will never be caught. As a matter fact, as soon as you think you have control, and you say that out loud, in any way, believing that you got a hold on life now, that's your challenge to God. And you know God loves a good challenge. In challenging God, you can here the umpire yelling, "Play ball!" and all your beliefs and ideas, your feelings and thoughts of having life all figured out are up for audit! So look out, because the game of life is on and the last ball gets thrown by you-know-who.

"You were never greater than you are right now, nor will you ever be. Your worth is already complete and never changes, only your relationship to it evolves."
-Michael Tamura

We so often react to the challenge of life until we find a better way, and until we find that better way, our healthier response lays dormant and we're stuck believing that we have to react to this world using old and habitual pathways of behavior. Truth be known, we can always imagine a different life. It's the knack of being human that's worth perfecting.

JOURNEY PROMPT

List two things you tend to react to spontaneously! (Without reason, irrationally, with anger or upset.) Now, ask yourself what a slower, more thoughtful, kinder, or more centered response might look like. In other words, how can you deal with that same situation with grace on your side?

**Self-betrayal is simple to explain.
It's not living from what we know to be our truth.**

"My goal is to be aware of the presence or non-presence of ill-will in my mind. The practice of loving kindness is the antidote to this."
-Sylvia Boorstein

JOURNEY PROMPT

"You've been walking in circles, searching. Don't drink by the water's edge. Throw yourself in. Become the water. Only then will your thirst end."
-Jeanette Berson

A simple question with hard answers: where in your life are you living outside your truth, personal power, or love?

When all is said and done and, finally, we've fully stepped into this life, we sit in admiration of our true beauty and the beauty that surrounds us. Inspired, we suddenly see the amazing wisdom of our existence. Stunned by its simple complexity, we are love, everything of this world is infinite, and we can't help but to feel into the miracle—a feeling which exists before any of our words. It's on this sacred ground of stunned silence where we can sit smiling forever, feeling the deepest understanding and appreciation of who we are here.

This journey back to ourselves is an eternal and sacred one, overwhelmingly beautiful to the mind and stunningly familiar to our heart. We're only asked to remember its purpose, which is to teach us love while we're here.

JOURNEY PROMPT

Try this exercise to help you see your thinking as simply a flow of energy. Sit back and listen to the conversation of the mind. Try not to be so attached to, intrigued by, or anxiously entertained by the content of your thinking. Just listen. Allow that stream of thoughts to flow through you without lingering on any of them. It's okay to view your thinking with passing curiosity. Most thoughts are simply experiments of the mind, and given permission, they flow on past. You can always come back and spark life into any one that you choose. Go for what feels good.

Remember: thinking that connects with your heart always feels perceivably different from the thinking that pulls you away from it.

"There comes a time when it is vitally important for your spiritual health to drop your clothes, look in the mirror, and say, 'Here I am. This is the body-like-no-other that my life has shaped. I live here. This is my soul's address."
-Barbara Brown Taylor

This world is an infinite collection of molecules, atoms, and subatomic particles that when broken down to their smallest parts are still infinite within themselves—all spectacular, never-ending miracles of existing form. The mere fact they exist at all is beyond anyone's cognitive understanding. As a matter of fact, even the concept of a realm, a dimension, and space-time awareness are existing miracles that are themselves beyond miraculous.

So then, how about *our* creation, *our* crazy human-spirited existence? And, on top of that, functioning within a space-time realm that is already an infinitely abundant miracle itself? Can't you see that you're a miracle within a miracle within a miracle? And the truly amazing thing is that even within this impossible reality, you can expand your consciousness even more, infinitely and forever—this is God's blessing on your already amazingly abundant and miraculous existence. Now that seems like a pretty big wow! Do I hear a WOW!?

JOURNEY PROMPT

Take a good look at anything physical in this world, animal or mineral, solid, gas, or liquid, and start dissecting it. And then look out into space and try and find an end to it. Look at the mind and find where a thought begins. If you believe in spirit, where is that? If you're able to look at any of these things and find a direction that doesn't keep going on forever, we need to have coffee. I want to know what and where that is!

Pay attention. Isn't this an amazing experience?

God didn't put me here to be rich, he put me here to be abundant!

God didn't put me here simply to be rich in material wealth, beautiful and perfect to look at, or important for the esteem and position of it, because I already am all that in ways that span far beyond the busy mind. God put me here filled, brilliant, and abundant!

> *"You find peace not by rearranging the circumstances of your life, but by realizing who you are at the deepest level."*
> -Eckhart Tolle

TRUTH IS TRUTH IS TRUTH IS TRUTH. The enlightenment we're all looking for is the same wisdom, understanding, love, and that higher state of being we've all been striving towards for millennia. We've been trying to teach and learn the secrets of the soul for thousands and thousands of years, but we tend to get caught up in our thinking, stuck in the business of our lives, dragged away by what we think we have to be doing first, distracted by our self-important ego world, and living our life through our pain and discomfort. Consequently, our inner world gets neglected and often shut down. It's almost as though it's easier for people to ignore their journey rather than accept it, but the lessons, challenges, pain, and irritations continue in an attempt to direct us back to the lessons and teachings we, in our truth, desire most—those which point us toward the realization of our selves.

JOURNEY PROMPT

Spend some personal time with these quotes and breathe into them:

"The greatest trap in our life is not success, popularity or power, but self-rejection."
-Henri Nouwen

"When we see our uniqueness as a virtue, only then are we at peace."
-Ghost in the Shell

You never left home base, you only believe you did. You started defining yourself through the whirling world instead of your own heart.

Seriously? You thought of that all by yourself?

Have you ever had a profound thought or an amazing idea about something, only to find that your beautiful, original thought is not new at all—that it's not just "your" idea, "your" thought, or "your" concept? It's something that's actually been conceived of before and maybe it's even been around in the world for a while, written on or spoken about by others, sometimes even by some very impressive people.

We all naturally tap into the same universal consciousness that feeds us our wisdom, it keeps us exploring and interacting with life at whatever level or phase of evolution human kind is ready to experience. Much of what we think about and explore in our heads has been thought of before by someone, and if it hasn't, and you do inspirationally think of something new (if that's possible), well, the world has apparently evolved to be able to express and handle that concept, and you're the one person who has been able to tap into that knowledge, that wisdom that has always been there, waiting.

In a way, you're kind of helping to push the evolution of the world's consciousness. You happened to tap into that particular frequency because you've been busy doing some wonderful personal work, consciously or subconsciously, with yourself, and you were able to throw some of your words around your inspiration. So, go with it, whether it seems old or new, it's new to you, and because no one will ever understand it exactly the way that you do, it's new to the world, and it can only add to the world's growth.

With billions of people in this world all connected to the common web of consciousness, it's inevitable that a few of us might come up with the same profound thought at a very similar point in time. We've been doing the same thing for thousands of years, all trying to touch the same light, evolve in the same way. So, walk with others gratefully on the journey, even if they're smarter, quicker, or write better than you! We're all here to learn huge and infinite lessons. We might as well help one another and do it together.

This journey is all ours!

This journey of learning to be gentler in a world that tends to pull us away from ourselves, of remembering the beauty within when we may not feel so beautiful, this journey of unfolding to the true nature of who we are, of connecting with the identity of love placed in our little hands, is the spirited search for an origin and a destiny that is eternal, timeless, and all ours to immerse ourselves in!

> *"Don't ask what the world needs. Ask what makes you come alive and go do it. Because what the world needs is people to come alive."*
> *-Howard Thurman*

JOURNEY PROMPT

Have you unnerved yourself? And what are you waiting for? Rumi says, "And you, when will you begin that long journey back to yourself?" He knew that we need to find our way back to our origin, like a child needs to find the breast. It's what nurtures our growth and, ultimately, what saves our life.

Do all the work you can to cultivate a higher state of consciousness for yourself! Your efforts simultaneously speak to others and helps draw the same out in them. It's as though your gift to yourself gives everyone permission to experience that same gift for themselves.

JOURNEY PROMPT

It's like a two-for-one sale! And what else are you going to do with your time here in this world? What else is worthy of a human life than doing the things that reflect and bring you towards the essence of your truth? Is there anything better to follow than your path towards expanding into higher levels of consciousness and love?

Over time, the aging process changes us. A life lived brings with it the slow repurposing of our bodies and our hearts. We make space for our metamorphosis by simply living our lives, hopefully with healthy intention and indulgence in the qualities of thinking that help us stay open to our more spirited identities.

These moments can happen at any time, however, biological menopause, in both women and men, seems to facilitate our movement toward ourselves. Utilizing this process of biological repurposing forces a physical and thus emotional shift as well as a recalibration of what we know to be important.

It makes sense that our misunderstanding of, or our resistance to, this natural process can create levels of personal and emotional discomfort with it, but opening to it in a peaceful way will serve us better on our journey.

Our world needs to honor aging, this mysterious gift of time, acknowledging that there is so much more to being human that lays beyond societies often distorted values and judgments of age. The mature heart is a time in one's life when it's safe to free our previously repressed pain, releasing it so that what wisdom lays behind can shine. There's an emergence of power and depth that can only move forward when we claim time as our partner.

Aging is nature's way of asking us to slowly relinquish our attachments to many of the qualities we believe identify who we are. We find identities through being a parent, a lover, a spouse, through procre-

ation and sexuality, our vocation, accomplishments, wealth, just to name a few. We find that everything we've identified ourselves through in the past can be set aside so that a real and true identity can come forward and re-establish itself on the fresh ground of time. As we age, we're asked to participate in life as we are now, in this moment, not as we were yesterday or thirty years ago. And we find our freedom in beginning again, starting fresh with a more experienced heart. A liberating, introspective question we can always ask ourselves is: Who am I now, today, in this moment? Yes, who am I now?

Our journey, our evolution in this world, signifies endings as well as beginnings. The aging process, at its best, brings with it deeper living and the expansive freedom of fresh and new life beyond the constraints of the material world. If we were to believe modern society's misinterpretation, that our natural aging is the end of life, well, that only creates confusion and suffering. In truth, aging signifies the strength of a new life, one based on who we are now, and moving infinitely closer to who we're meant to be.

Is this change in life energy simply our physical body's attempt at trading our desires and distractions in life for a deeper dedication to the journey? The body does indeed follow the mind, and when the mind naturally evolves, do we deny it, or when we're asked by time to follow it, do we smile to ourselves and say yes?

Perhaps by recalibrating the way we see our world we can find a quality of energy that suits our life journey better. We're drawn towards a way of being that allows us to honor our natural growth, a growth

derived simply by living as long as we have thus far. And does living also bring with it countless opportunities to begin again, to start a new life based from a place of fresh thought and heart? Is this not what time teaches us?

Life will slow you down so that you can do the work that you've avoided, put to the side through the years. Ask yourself, *What do I need to work on now in order to move forward today?* Use this time, this natural process of slowing down, and ask what life is trying to bring to you now, what life wants of you now.

Why not use these natural processes of life to help you move into your deepest and most personal growth? Why not allow it to bring you where you've always wanted to go? Don't you think that's what it's meant for? We're always striving against life, as though we should be perfect specimens for 100 years. But we are, we just need to re-evaluate how we categorize that.

Every decade, every five years, every year brings a new quality to who we are. We have a whole new world to negotiate. Why would we do it under the premise of being forever young? Why would we do it using old data to program a new computer?

Trying to live at the same capacity that we did ten, twenty, even thirty years ago is bizarre behavior when you think about it. There's no reason that all the things that we had decades prior would be available to us now, and there's so much that we should have grown past as well. We need to become familiar with the phrase, "That's not who I am any-

more," we need to give ourselves the space to step back and say, "Who am I today? How do I walk forward as a 45-year-old or a 55-year-old or a 65-year-old? What's appropriate for me now?" Because what was appropriate before no longer applies in many profound ways to who we are today. Honor your process, always walk forward, open to who you are now.

It's interesting how similar the symptoms of andropause and menopause are for both men and women. Here are just a few:

- Irritability and mood swings (impatience with the ways of an irrational world)

- Hot flashes (endocrine changes, signaling deeper shifting within the emotional body)

- Fatigue (the misuse of the body, trying to strive to live at a different age)

- Lower sex drive (identifying yourself not through sexuality but through heart, no use for that quality of survival energy)

- Distracted or poor concentration (finding greater importance in the heartfelt and less cognitive things of life)

- Increased body fat (physical drive decreased, meditative and contemplative life naturally increased)

We all use different qualities of variations in our language, slang or learned dialects of speech, that speak more clearly to us—approaches to language appropriate for who we are. To define the different ways things might look when it comes to bringing us back to love only adds value to our journey. Different ways of speaking can change how we see things, and different people will need to use different language. For example, a friend of mine once said, "I did her a solid." Until I had a second to think about it, I had no clue what she was saying. After it sunk in and I realized it had nothing to do with constipation, I realized it was a good, honorable act of strength she was talking about. So, "Do yourself a solid." Remember love, remember your love, and remember you're love. Spend a little time figuring out the best ways to say it for you.

Return over and over to the journey phrases that work for you. What language do you need to use to effectively surround the concept of reclaiming your truth? Make it up if you have to, use your slang, find an old phrase that works. Just grab onto something that works, at least for now. That's one of your power statements, that's a "solid" to walk through life with, for now.

JOURNEY PROMPT
Multiple Choice:

The phrases below are different ways we can speak to the concept of willingly releasing our blockages and resistance to the presence of love in our journey. Choose one of these similar phrases that speaks to you, or make up your own:

    A. Shed the beliefs that limit your understanding that love is real, and love is accessible.

    B. Stop screwing around and just love one another!

    C. I will learn how to shed any beliefs which limit my ability to see that love is alive within me.

    D. _____ (fill in the blank, this one's all yours!)

    E. I touch and honor this world by releasing fear and embracing my awareness of the presence of love within me.

    F. Okay, world, I'm open! Show me the LOVE!

    G. "Be the love you wish to see in the world." -Ghandi

"There is one spectacle grander than the sea, that is the sky; there is one spectacle grander than the sky, that is the interior of the soul."
-Victor Hugo

Our self-judgment, negativity, and questionable self-worth can be distracting as we attempt to reclaim ourselves and remember our truth. So often, we end up viewing ourselves as broken and needing to be fixed, but, in truth, we're not broken, and there's nothing about us that we need to fix. We're put here to do the work of life and to participate in the world embracing what comes forward. That's the whole point. Making mistakes, fumbling and struggling through different aspects of life doesn't require us to look down at ourselves, or see ourselves as flawed, it only asks us to see our human vulnerability and recognize what it is to offer ourselves grace. And when we can do this, when we can love what we are and not see ourselves as alien, or failed, it automatically sets us up to do the same with each other.

We do, however, need to pay attention to our state of wellbeing. We need to continuously attend to the quality our thinking, to stay on track in a world that we can get easily distracted in. With a breath of understanding and compassion, we need to remember what and who we are so that we can maintain our touch point with the spirited memory of our truth that sparks our hearts.

JOURNEY PROMPT

How often are we distracted drivers while we travel the highways of this world? In a car, being distracted is dangerous and can kill people. Inside ourselves, distracted driving pulls us away from our awareness of who we really are. In either situation, it's best to view the distractions that tempt our attention with a light, almost passing interest while maintaining our greater attention on what's in front of us now.

Ruminations on Peace

Our journey inevitably leads us back to recalibrating ourselves to a vibratory state that reflects a truth whose nature mirrors its creator. That peace is our natural inheritance. Our suffering, meant to be temporary, teaches us what it must and evaporates under the pressure of love, it gives peace the space and character to live within us.

This is the work of life, of remembering our spirited identity. It's a commitment to something far, far greater than ourselves—and yet, it is us—this journey back to love is what makes us what we are.

As you create peace in your walking world, take the time to define it in your mind:
- What does it look like to be at peace within your walking world?
- What does it feel like within your heart to be at peace?
- Who would you be if you walked with more peace?

Being aware and catching yourself when you slip or, even better, before you slip, that's the greatest tool of all, it's our jack hammer of self-awareness.

Try to avoid "reacting" to events. Wait until you can respond with clear and healthy intention. This requires you to move in life from a place of peace, to know compassion and forgiveness, and hold the essence of them close in your heart before attempting any discussion of a difficult or painful sort.

Choose well, and be patient with your process, because your journey toward peace lasts a lifetime.

I find people who are willing, even enthusiastic, to admit their mistakes and use them as a learning tool for others as well as for themselves to be quite inspiring. A great example of this is Maya Angelou's book *Letter to My Daughter*. She discusses different aspects of life, and isn't scared to touch the multiple mistakes she's made in the social world she's lived in. In the book, she freely talks about times when she's assumed or judged things to be not as they truly were. She talks about moments when she's caught herself making mistakes and the emotional cost to her in the moment, and goes on to discuss how those mistakes helped to develop her character, her courage, and her strength.

This is a quality of self-actualization worth striving for. We're all worthy of embracing those moments, the mistakes, the judgments and lack of character that we've fallen into at times rather than ruminating on them as mistakes, and seeing ourselves as less because of them; learning the lessons rather than turning away from them in fear.

I am not my emotional landscape.

*I am not my blood sugar, my hormones,
my income, or my good and bad relationships.*

*I am not my arguments or my opinions,
my possessions or my poverty.*

I am not my struggles or even my joys.

*I am on my journey, and all my experiences,
they are vitally a part of it.*

*I am remembering who I am, not defining by
the world, but remembering through it.*

*And, oh, what a humanly bumpy-smooth road
that can be!*

And still I hold sacred space within,

*I honor that songbird in my heart that sounds
its ancient song...*

I am Spirit. I am Peace. I am Love.

JOURNEY PROMPT

It's a hard row to hoe in this world, not to get taken in by all its diversions, distracted to the point of anxiety by the attention-grabbing emotions, pleasures, and dramas. We're doing well if we're not getting completely absorbed, losing ourselves in their theatrical antics. Try not to get overtaken by it all. All the potholes, the shiny temptations and stories of life aren't supposed to own you, they just teach you different ways to dance to your own music. We're not meant to live by them, they teach us how to free our hearts through them.

So, find the balance of interacting with your life that feeds you, avoiding getting lost in all the desires, emotions and dramas, while embracing them enough to know they're also an essential part of your human experience. They do, indeed, make up part of your journey, they just don't define it. Let yourself live through the experience, not in it. Let yourself experience it all, to know and understand what life offers this human form, and, remember, it doesn't run the show. All these experiences and distractions are not meant to pull us away from ourselves, they're meant to show us ourselves.

"You are the sky. Everything else, it's just the weather."
-Pema Chödrön

Your power statement: I am the sky, everything else is simply the weather.

**I'm tired of getting stuck in my ego
at the expense of living my life.**

Thinking back, chiropractic college had to have been the most ego-directed time of my life. Those years were tough, a time when connecting to my heart proved wrenchingly hard. I was stuck in fear and egotistical thinking, simultaneously wrapped up in the need to be good enough and scared of not being enough. Questioning and comparing myself socially, academically, spiritually and personally. It was a great recipe for cooking up a great big pot of personal hell! And I succeeded! I wasn't a good student, wasn't a good friend or partner, hadn't yet developed the habits and qualities I needed to build my life on. I had created a nightmare for myself. Life had me by the shorthairs, to say the least. Everything felt tenuous at best, healthy relationships of all kinds were far and few between. Family, well, they tolerated me, begrudgingly.

Potentially, I could've done a better job. But think I knew I was missing some wrenches in the tool kit. I was so stuck that I never felt like I had what I needed to find my way out of a life I had created. At that point in my life, I was doing my best with what I had, I just didn't have very much. I just didn't have the evolution of spirit to choose better, I didn't yet know a better way. I've heard that in ancient times, the Japanese believed that a drunk person was not held responsible for their actions because they were not capable of knowing better in their inebriated state. Well, I was drunk, and I was in Japan.

But knowing better, that's something that takes time. It's some-

thing that's somewhat age appropriate, at least for the spirit, and what can I say? I'm a slow learner, a slow processor, so sometimes, for me, life's lessons are learned slower than for the average bear, kind of like trying to watch a snail do Michael Jackson's moonwalk. The big lessons seem to take me forever to get. But I've been out of school for over thirty years now and I think I have a better grip on things. Wait a minute, and let me ask my office manager if that's true… What? Oh! Um…Well, never-mind. And I continue!

People just want to be given permission to remember who they are, to become more.

We create all kinds of stories, scenarios, and dramas in an attempt to cultivate and grasp that permission, but the truth is, we already have it. We don't need to receive anyone's permission. We already are that which we seek. We already are more, we just need to give ourselves permission to see it and be it.

When the understanding of our true nature brings us to a place of peace, we know we've remembered an authentic truth about ourselves deep within. We know that we've taken a wonderful leap forward in this journey toward self-awareness.

When we understand that we're all human, we're all walking a similar path, and doing our best to live our lives in a way that reflects our spiritual nature, it helps us see the world surrounding everyone with a freshness that tends to be more fulfilling to the heart and far less fear-provoking to the mind.

Sometimes we need to get to the point in life where we realize that the issues we encounter almost always fall into the category "issues-in-process." Our challenges aren't wired like a light switch, so easy to turn on or off. They're more like a slow-moving—mind-numbingly slow—and relentlessly sensitive dimmer switch that has a habit of re-setting itself. Our funny little issue switches require us to establish our habits of repeatedly reinforcing our new patterns of thought and behavior in order to consciously move closer to our healing.

I'm committed to allowing something different into my life, striving for something more beautiful to come through me. It's what I desire, what I need, it's the journey I'm here for. To be better, uncontrolled by my urges and issues. I'm here to do the work that's required. I'm here to be love.

JOURNEY PROMPT

So remember, this journey toward love is not an on/off switch. It's more like a dimmer switch, one that's slowly, sometimes imperceptibly, adjusted, but, in the end, creates a quality of unexpected brightness. Be patient with your process, be persistent and consistent, redirecting, adjusting, fine-tuning yourself, and breathe into each moment. See how wonderful life can be right now. Live to notice your unexpected light.

"It is our privilege and our adventure to discover our own special light."
-Mary Dunbar

We all start as the same bright spirit of love. We are all the same no matter how we might look to each other in this moment. We began in this world completely aware of our spirit, until we touched down in this formed world. That bright spot didn't evaporate, but it did get reorganized, covered over with the treasured shroud of being human.

"Until we learn to love the most difficult parts of ourselves, we can't really be free to love in this world."
-Gandhi

There's a love that creates and holds us together, a love that flies beyond all of our beliefs about love, a love that defines the inner workings of what we are, a love that reflects all that we deeply yearn to be. This is the love of you. It doesn't require anything but your being. Others are optional here, things unnecessary, and everything benefits from your presence in this place. Be your love in its deepest forms, in all the infinite forms that love unfolds through you. If you do nothing else in this world, be your love.

Affirmation:

As you take a heart-centered breath, allow each line of this affirmation to flow through you and pay attention to the ones that you resonate with. Linger in it and absorb its message into your heart.

I am breath.
I am divine breath.
I am breathed by the divine.
The divine breath rises through me.
The breath of divine love flows through me.
The divine breathes through me, and I breathe life for the divine.

How do you get from the head to the heart?

Through having gratitude, no matter what, regardless of the circumstance you find yourself in.

Even when you believe that the people around you are negative, have gratitude for them. They have added to your world in ways that you or they may not be aware of yet. It doesn't mean you have to participate in their negativity, it only means that they're human (and there's deep purpose to their presence). There are no human enemies, there are just people in pain asking for help.

Be in the big, big, big wow of life, the never-ending wow of paying attention to the infinite miracles that run through you, surround you, engulf your view.

What is it to use the developmentally appropriate words of heart? I find that what I do is put the appropriate language into concepts that are typically more difficult, intellectualized, and approached with possibly a bit of hubris. Life is simple, the words we use to describe it, they need to be simple, easy to grasp, appropriate for a heart-centered state.

And at the end of a seminar, a teacher was asked, "What is the meaning of life?" The teacher took a mirror and caught the reflection of the sun, shined it into the student's face and said, "Our job, the very meaning of life, is to find the light within and to shine it wherever we can, to define dark spaces and brighten them, to add to the light of others, and to reflect it back into ourselves, allow it to open doors we never knew we could open." The student asked, "Do you have a reference for that?" And the teacher smiled.

> *"Compassion for others begins with kindness to ourselves."*
> *-Pema Chodron*

When we fill so much of our space with our judgment—judgment of ourselves, of one another, and of this world—that we forget to truly celebrate this life and forget what it is to feel and be present in our sadness, we lose that part of ourselves that makes us very human.

And if you can find your own beautiful way to walk through this world without judgement, people will think you're missing something. They don't see you reacting and reaching out in your old ways, behaving like you used to, being like them. In their eyes, you might even look dulled or complacent. But without judgment, you're free to be yourself without the desire to judge, without your need to live only to please those around you, to entertain their opinions. And you're free not to feel compelled to control everyone and everything around you. So, in reality, you really are missing something. You're missing that part of yourself that was so wrapped up in your thinking, fear, anxious reactions, and your judgments that you truly forgot who you were. You're missing defining yourself through a paradigm that's not you, but one that you received from society and the people around you. You're free from negating your own truth, covering your own love, and you can finally walk in this world, rediscovering yourself every moment of every day.

Only focusing on love won't necessarily fix the problems that we have in this world, but really focusing on love as it relates to this world and how we live in it will absolutely help us find better approaches to our problems. It opens us up to better solutions when we can get greed and fear out of the way. We remember the most important part of being human is that we can love, and find our success through that love, and that, that's always a better way to live.

Love. It's not born of the busy head, not an intellectual process we need to "figure out." Love is born through our creation, in that moment placed preciously and gently in our heart. It's a quality of who we are that we need only to learn to be present to. The mind's job is to receive the hearts whisper, its knowledge and wisdom. And this is where the lessons and figuring out begins. Here, with a breath, we learn how to walk forward with the gift that our heart presents to the world. It's here, in listening to the whisper of our heart, that we find our peace.

Above all, we're here to explore LOVE in all its forms.

Stepping back and taking a look at all this anxiety that we allow ourselves to get caught up in, our tension about what's going on in our lives or with its unknowable future, or the multiple ways we come up with to struggle with one another, the rights and the wrongs, the good and the bad judgments we hold, not to mention what we do to ourselves. And there's all the life events and happenings that we anguish over, seemingly unable to work through them and let go and move on. Our management of this struggle can all be summed up in the simple statement: no matter what our experience in this life, no matter what's thrown our way or isn't, our biggest issue, the one that supersedes them all will always come down to the fact that **we don't want to die before we learn to love.** That scares us, and it keeps us living through our fear rather than through what we desire most: to live through our love.

Living through our love, that's the juice of the journey, the biggest fish to fry; that's where our attention belongs, it's what we have to negotiate in our world, stepping beyond life's drama and towards the love we wish to know. It's a dilemma that ends up being the root of most of our struggle—our desire to learn love. And as much as we yearn for it, it gets hidden under all the distractions and dramas of life that only keeps us from embracing our higher goal.

We do seem to get in our own way. Maybe we're just putting ourselves through every imaginable antic and ordeal we can find, trying to push the subject of recognizing love through forcing ourselves to look

deeply into the eyes of its opposite, subconsciously turning up the heat on the topic because we haven't been taught, or figured out how to find our love without first communicating with its evil twin, tension. If that's true, all we can hope for is that we're fast learners, that we can prevent our death until after we find our love, because it would sure be nice to know that we caught that "golden ring" in all its forms before the ride is over.

So, do your best to put all the small stuff to the side, even the things you think rank for attention can probably be re-categorized, and then step back and recognize what exists largest within you, in the core of what you are, in your heart, and try not to make finding love so hard to remember.

Take the journey:
Live love before you die so you're not forced to die before you let yourself really live. **Find your love.**

> *"When we know better, we do better."*
> –Maya Angelou

"Knowing better" can erupt in a miraculous kind of way that surprises us with wisdom and a common sense not always easily accessible when we're stuck in ill will of any kind. It's a spark from within, moving outward into all our doings—an epiphany of change, a shift away from old paradigms and dogmas whose fear no longer works and is no longer welcome, and it's all for the sake of living in more love. Knowing better may start in the mind as an attempt to understand the confusion of life, but its grand finale always takes place in the heart, and our full embrace of doing better is dependent on that finale. We cannot own "better" until "better" is known from within.

If you're resisting the statement, "When we know better, we do better," then go deeper. Ask yourself what moving through life immersed in the wisdom of the heart looks like. Can we ever go against our love when we use only that as our guide?

Sometimes we just have to get out of our heads about what life has presented to us and settle into our hearts about it. It's here that we find the secret of what it is to know something better so that we can make our choice to live a better way. Without connecting to our heart, this better way would be impossible to grasp.

Sometimes we have to get out of our heads about what life has presented to us and settle into it through our hearts. It's here that we find the secret of what it is to know something better and in that we make

our choices to do better. Without perfecting our art of connecting to life through the heart, our better way would be impossible to access.

When we know better through our heart, we automatically do better. But that requires going to a deeper place of knowing not frequently explored.

JOURNEY PROMPT
Where in your life would it be helpful if you could find that better way of doing and being? Hint: consider any area of judgment, anger, resentment, jealousy, anguish, or struggle of any kind.

> *"There came a time when the risk to remain tight in the bud was more painful than the risk it took to blossom."*
> *—Anaïs Nin*

When we're no longer concerned about how the conditions of our life relate to our happiness, we gain a freedom that overpowers any desire to have someone else create happiness for us.

JOURNEY PROMPT

If you've ever, in any way, lost a friend, you know it changes your life. But it doesn't stop it. Friends, family, mothers, fathers, lovers, acquaintances may leave, they may have to, but our happiness will continue to evolve as a reflection of us living through our own heart—it's the only place happiness can truly move through us, we don't ever really get it from anyone else.

"Love does not dominate, it cultivates."
-Johann Wolfgang von Goethe

When you get to the point where you realize that there is actually nothing more important than love, suddenly, you look at everything that you have been striving for, trying to acquire, desiring to control, and none of it seems quite as important as maintaining that status of love from within. Does it matter if you have money, power, or status if you don't have love?

Can you come up with any adequate replacement or good excuse for avoiding being the love that exists within you?

JOURNEY PROMPT

Make a list of all the things in life that are more important than knowing love. (Yup, it's gonna be an impossibly short list!)

When we no longer define ourselves through secondary identities—our contrived and inherited stories about how much or what we have, what we drive, what we do, our stories of addiction, health, and life problems, our judgment of good and bad behavior, our sexuality, and the list goes on and on—in releasing our identification with our stories, we open to and create real and new freedom in our lives.

When we refuse to identify ourselves through our stories and dramas, it helps us free our minds, thus opening ourselves to new ways of experiencing who we are, experiencing a spirited and authentic life closer to the heart because, suddenly, we are not what we've done or what's been done to us. We've stepped beyond that, we're identified by an internal essence based in love—a sacred truth that becomes amplified in and through our hearts.

There's so much to gain from living beyond our stories:

- Interactions with others become more natural and loving.

- As we live in our own light, we see everyone around us with a fresher light as well. We see people as spirited humans doing their best rather than as problems or objects. We see others as the same as us rather than above or below us.

- We become free to simply be ourselves without any preconceived notions or unrealistic assumptions—wonderfully free from the disappointment associated with expectations about anyone, including ourselves.

- We step into life with a greater sense of truth, honor, humor, and spirit, open to our own higher levels of love.

When we no longer define ourselves through what we do, what we want to do, or have done, we invite into our lives a fresh new world that was previously unavailable.

JOURNEY PROMPT

Pick any story that you've attached to with identity and look for the truth of it. Can that story really define you? For example: I love photography. I participate in it all the time, and sometimes I call myself a "photographer." However, when the rubber meets the road, this is simply a personal interest that I find some level of life expression through. If there were no cameras, I would still be me—an expression of light. Nothing overrides that. No matter how hard we hold onto our secondary stories, they can never define us. And I can't even begin to tell you how the story "I'm divorced" doesn't define my essence or my heart.

**Beware of giving unsolicited advice.
Love detaches itself from judging how we think others should be.**

Free everyone from your opinions about them! It simultaneously liberates you and them from the trap of your judgment. In that same vein of thought, never hold anyone a prisoner of your prejudice, your assumptions about them, or the tendency to take them personally. We all struggle, we all make mistakes, we're all trying to figure out this often painful world as best as we can, and we could all benefit from a little help, some compassion and understanding from one another.

These statements of patience and compassion with one another are brave statements to make on your journey, and worthy ones to confront within yourself. As long as it's not dangerous or harmful to anyone, allow people to make their own choices, allow them to be themselves without your unsolicited advice and judgment. Allow them their lessons—after all, they're theirs to learn, and if they happen to want advice then they'll find a way to ask for it. Otherwise, most of your opinions and judgments are really none of your business anyway. It's probably best to use your mind in stronger ways.

JOURNEY PROMPT

To know when to speak and when not to can be a bit of an art. I have a friend who loves the phrase, "Your opinion about me is none of my business." She knows how to keep her thinking clean, centered on her path toward loving herself and others, and not distracted by any unnecessary opinions. Another way to approach our judgment and personalized opinions about others can look like this: Once you catch yourself, stop and say to yourself, "My opinion, my judgment of you and about you is none of my business. I wish you well." This helps us suspend our judgment and encourages us to cultivate new qualities of thinking that build us all up rather than depleting us.

We could all use a little of that. So, who do we become when we free ourselves from destructive opinions, whether they belong to us or someone else?

"Your task is not to seek for love, but merely to seek and find all the barriers within yourself that you have built against it."
-Jalaluddin Rumi

Huge point: We can always choose new, choose better, choose more love. A gentler life always exists already, you just have to be willing to touch it.

In large part, the thinking that naturally flows through us can usually be gentler, softer, less aggressive, and far less anxious. There's a trickle of possible thoughts always flowing through our minds that we can pay attention to or choose not to. Learn to recognize where your attention is and understand where you're stuck, then open to and look for your gentler, more peaceful way. This is the space where your wisdom can reclaim you and you can claim it.

JOURNEY PROMPT

Periodically monitor how your mind is doing at any particular moment. Pay attention to the quality of thinking you're in and present yourself with the question: "Do I need to tweak this a bit?"

The answers are usually pretty clear: "Yup! Probably should!" Or, "Nope, feels good, feels pretty clear right now."

The reason things come up over and over again is because we haven't figured out how to see them in a loving way yet. We're just not finished with that topic. This doesn't define anything about who you are. It just simply lets you know there's more work to be done.

JOURNEY PROMPT

It's our ability to love something that sets everything free. It's where our healing lays and that's where we find our strength.

But how do you see things in a more loving way? How do we know when we're there? There has to be a softening of preconceived notions, and that requires you to open up to seeing things differently from wherever and whatever disconcerting thought you're stuck with in the moment. In attitudes of love, there's an improved state of ease that overtakes any situation. In this space, we can be with what we know and be open to seeing the situation differently. We can attach to the other aspects of love, like compassion and kindness, understanding, forgiveness, tenderness, a deeper sense of personal strength, and healthy justice. All of these qualities might have been previously unavailable to you in any real way. Their fuller presence lets you know that love, in all its beauty and strength, has emerged through you.

Remember:
Frequent and repetitive reinforcement of a new energetic pattern is essential for change. *If you want love, continuously reinforce what love is inside of you over and over and over until you can't stand it anymore! And then, do it again! Wash, rinse, repeat. Wash, rinse, repeat…*

JOURNEY PROMPT

In learning anything new—a language, any academic subject, a sport, a way of thinking—it requires practice. We have to immerse ourselves in anything that we really want to fully grow into. This is true for love, compassion, non-judgment, all of the lessons of life that we long for need repeated reinforcement in order for us to own them. It never happens all at once, like a download from the matrix. If you want to learn a new language, reinforce it through practice. If you're trying to learn a sport, again, practice. It takes a lifetime of practice in order to become great or even good at anything. This applies to *all* the questions of the journey. How do I become more loving? How can I walk in this world with more compassion? How can I find a way to eliminate judgment from my life? How can I be more kind? How can I not take things personally? How can I not allow fear to rule my world? How can I be free of the good opinions of others? How can I eat better? How can I drink more water? How can I stop drinking? How can I be nicer? And so on. The answers are all based in having the willingness to practice your desire over and over again until you become what you know is your truth. You already are what you seek. It just needs plenty of reinforcement.

Believing in the best of someone requires truth and the strength of love to be present.

"The art of love is largely the art of persistence."
-Albert Ellis

JOURNEY PROMPT

When we allow ourselves to believe in the best of who somebody can be, especially someone we care about, it automatically sets us up to release the judgments we've made about them, and it allows us to explore forgiveness with that person. We find within ourselves a place where we're not willing to identify people through their mistakes and bad choices.

You're not condoning their past deeds and behaviors, and you're not tolerating any more inappropriate behavior from them, but you're choosing to see them as more than their mistakes, more than their past issues—the same way you would want to be seen.

When we look for the best of who another person can be, we're able to let go of our negative judgment, preconceptions, and stories that we've surrounded and imprisoned them with, often at our own expense.

After this, our questions become: How should we see the people we struggle with as we step past our fear and our judgment about them? How can we safely open our hearts to allow kindness, justice based in truth, compassion, and the strength of love to come forward?

Your ability to take care of yourself in a loving way naturally reflects towards the people you love, and even towards the ones you think you don't!

JOURNEY PROMPT

People pay attention. You might not think they do, but they do, and even the ones that aren't exactly wishing you well still learn from your example. It touches them when you walk forward with love. They may not know it right away, but it has an impact, and it's up to them to do something with it. Your love pretty much ends with you. It's not your job to tell anyone else how to live, what to pay attention to, or how to love, but it is your job to live life from a place that's beautiful.

Our entire journey is woven together with lessons of love: learning to be more gentle, understanding, and compassionate with ourselves and others; learning to listen to those in need, to be kind, strong, and just in what's right, and learning to free ourselves from our own judgment. We are all journeying forward to find that often hidden and deepest capacity that we know exists within for a love we hold in our core. In this lays our origin and our destiny. It is our beginning and our end. Love is our journey.

"Love is the bridge between you and everything."
-Rumi

JOURNEY PROMPT

Create a list of power statements for yourself that reflect lessons of love. Find quotes, statements, and words that keep you in the spirit of love, that maintain you in the essence that is your truth.

Ways to remember that our journey is love:

1) Ex: *"There is no path to peace. Peace is the path." -Mahatma Gandhi*

2) Ex: *"If only your eyes saw souls instead of bodies, how very different our ideals of beauty would be." -Unknown*

3)

4)

The Sufi's have a saying:
"The heart that can't be broken is not a true heart anyway, so break me, now."

Being stubbornly stuck in fear, anger, confusion, frustration, and difficult emotional issues are indicator lights that tell you it's important to reboot your thinking and re-calibrate your nervous system. In any disruptive attachment to negative emotions, you need to step back from participating in them as well as the actions they produce, and rewire your brain so that you can approach the situation differently. "Differently" often means with more self-compassion and a deeper self-love. These are the qualities that help free you from attachments to negativity.

JOURNEY PROMPT

To find solutions, sometimes we need to shut down the current program and reload another—one that's love-based, not based in an old fear mentality. Then, we need to busy ourselves applying new thought to old situations.

1. Hold yourself close to love, because that's where your strength resides.

"When you arise in the morning, think of what a precious privilege it is to be alive—to breathe, to think, to enjoy, to love."
-Marcus Aurelius

JOURNEY PROMPT

This is a wonderful concept, this living fully present in our love, seeing the privilege of the gift, embracing our life. And depending on what's happening in our life or our mind, there are always those days where it might not be so easy to get there. So here's a little morning ritual:

>Before you get out of bed, take a moment and visualize the new ways you want to walk in this world. Rebuild what you want your life to look like and spend some time before your feet ever hit the ground visualizing and manifesting that. Dream of what that would look like, and who you would be in this new world. See your truth and deny space to your lies in this day. Wake up to your morning and your gift of "alive."

Like Jimmy Buffett says in his song *Fruitcakes*:
"Now here comes the big ones. Relationships!
We all got 'em, we all want 'em. What do we do with 'em?"

What gives us more potential for growth than our relationships? What gives us more headaches, more joy, more passion, more pain, more alive vitality, and more heart-wrenching burnout? Nothing gives us more fuel for the fire of the journey than our relationships, especially those magnetic ones, rich with our ideas of love!

JOURNEY PROMPT

What would it take and how might it influence your life if Nouwen's quotes were guidelines for our relationships? Include everyone, your partner, children, friends, any family members, even your casual acquaintances and less-than-friends.

"There's no such thing as boundless love,
you need to have healthy boundaries."

"The task: claim yourself for yourself so that you can contain
your needs within the boundaries of yourself and hold them
within the presence of those you love."

"True mutuality in love requires people who possess themselves and
who can give to each other while holding onto their own identities."
-Henri J.M. Nouwen

Start accumulating your **Power Statements For Love.** Write them down and look at them regularly. It's so easy to get sidetracked away from healthy love. We have to remind ourselves over and over again what love looks like to the healthy heart.

We develop a pretty thick crust of anxiety around us the longer we choose to stay in a position or attitude of fear.

JOURNEY PROMPT
So, how would you like to handle that?

Hint: There's an antidote to fear. It lays in trust, love, compassion, plus all of the other building blocks of our authentic and most true identity.

I'm hardest on the people I think have the most potential. Especially the ones that spend their moments getting in their own way, sabotaging what they can be, rather than opening to their amazing unfolding life, living their talents, remembering their hearts.

This thought was an inspired epiphany for me: I think the loss, the non-realization of our potential is the greatest wrong we can commit against ourselves, and not encouraging the potential in one another, well, that's even worse. We're put in this world with such vast abundance, and to not take advantage of the gift, that one time, never-to-return-again-ever gift, well, when you think about it, it's almost ludicrous not to. It's us choosing to believe in our inability to express the potential we were graced with rather than believing in what we can be that I find deeply and painfully disappointing. So, I'm especially hard on those I believe in most, which is usually those that are closest to me. But it's not just about them. Everybody in this world has huge potential, and I think the loss of believing in that potential is perhaps the greatest crime a human could commit towards themselves or inspire in another.

JOURNEY PROMPT

I'm not trying to talk specifically about politics or religion in this entry, but politics as well as religion serve as strong examples of how groups that have a broad common goal tend to fracture and splinter into smaller groups that get caught up in their need to be seen as right or special, losing their ability to see and act on the big picture, the primary ideas they have in common. They lose track of their common, more universal understanding and wisdom. And it does seem logical that if we were just

able to keep our attention on what we all have in common rather than getting caught up in our differences, all of us individualistic and grouped-up humans would naturally get along better. Its so easy for us to lose ourselves in who's right and who's wrong and, in the process, lose track of the bigger, far more important idea. When we can admit that, it opens us up to healing from the heartbreak of feeling separated and different from one another. So I think this concept, at the very least, is worth thinking about:

The core of most religion seems to embody searching for the best way to remember our love while in human form. At their core, most religions seem to base their identity in the overriding backdrop of understanding love.

But in a more superficial and ego-driven mode, most religions tend to develop a bigger agenda, they want to inspire their own unique way of practice, insisting and sometimes even forcing, passively or aggressively, their particular flavor of "wisdom" on the participant.

It's likely that our American political system evolved in much the same way: The parties were born as equalizers, meant to represent different approaches and ideas of moving towards the same ultimate goal, one of helping the population of America thrive, a way to give everyone opportunities to live with personal strength and freedom. They're all trying to find the best way to cultivate human capacity in this world, to help inspire the best participation of everyone. Ultimately, they all want the same thing: capacity for human success. But all the fractured and broken political parties seem to have lost track of the bigger truth of what they're

meant to be. They've swapped their honorable ideas, becoming stuck in an egotistical journey that will doing anything to win an election, despite what builds the people.

Everyone desires the highest expression of our human potential. So whether it's about the individual or the group, it's about the sanctity of human expression, and, at our core, that's what we've always been about. The argument's not about whether or not our largest truth gets seen, it's about the technique we use, what it takes to get it seen.

I find myself asking: How are religious or political organizations different from how we treat one another daily? Don't we also distort our original message the same as religions and political parties do when we're not paying attention to living through our hearts? We effect the world just like religion and politics, they just have their effect on larger swathes of the population.

When we try to control everyone, pushing and persuading them to see life the same as we do, when we let our ego dictate its judgment rather than listening to our heart-centered goals, we create an environment where huge problems and arguments tend to evolve for us.

Letting our desire to be right, the need to believe that we know what's best, can control our world disrupts the very heart of who we are. We end up creating chaos and judgment that leads to living life in a world where we just can't seem to get along with each other. We're too busy looking fearfully at the other guy or group. Whether it's an individual or a group, when we can find the space to see that we all basically want the

same thing, an honest opportunity for human expression and love, but we just have different ways of asking for it, it leaves us a place for negotiation, a place to be with one another, a place to accept our differences.

> *"It is not our differences that divide us. It is our inability to recognize, accept and celebrate those differences."*
> *-Audre Lorde*

The Happy Sacrificial Lamb!

We're all participants in one another's journey. Each playing a role for the benefit of one another and for ourselves. When we can see past any drama and attachment to our stories, it allows us to be grateful to one another for the underlying and unknowable sacrifice we each make for one another's growth.

We all participate and play roles in each other's lives for the sole purpose of helping one another wake up to ourselves. It might seem like we're just driving one another insane, or exercising our hidden agendas, or that we're simply trying to be in a relationship with one another or just get along working together, but there's always more to it than that! This life and all its events are far bigger then the simplicity we tend to attach to them. We're here to create opportunities in whatever way we can to see our own magnificence and show one another theirs! Here to help one another heal, remember the full awesomeness of love we were created with! To look in astonishment through the head of that needle we did the back stroke through to get to rediscover our paradise-lost!

As we step up to life's lessons, whatever they may be, and however they might be disguised, our fellow players will push us and challenge us to remember our truth and lean towards our love. Their participation in our journey, whether gentle or harsh, acts as a guide that challenges us to see our light beyond the darkness of life's burdens. In a sense, we owe them a debt of gratitude, even though it rarely feels like that in the moment. They come with hidden gifts, always. We have to be willing to

see life in that light.

At a deeper spirited level that we rarely acknowledge, we're all sacrificing for one another in this life, immersed in a great effort to move toward our truth, with and for one another. No one promised us an easy passage, just an amazing potential for a fruitful one. Pay attention to your opportunities to move forward with love; they abound always.

There's always bigger purpose behind any experience that we have in life, unseen lessons and meaning within every event we find ourselves negotiating. Our journey asks us to look for that purpose and open to its message.

It's impossible for us to always know or see all the the deeper, even hidden, roles that any interaction may hold for us, to grasp some understanding of the life lesson being thrown to us. These lessons naturally come as a result of being awake and curious to our experiences, staying open to all their potential gifts, the teachings that these struggles as well as joys might offer. It profits us on this journey to stay dedicated to our open minds, loyal to our willingness to explore life always deeper, even in the midst of strong emotional distractions. So be mindful of the potential opportunities that get presented to us in every moment of life. These opportunities are brought in to help us expand ourselves, meant to help us evolve and build our lives with. There's no situation presented to us that can't help us remember ourselves, that ultimately isn't meant to encourage us, to stretch us toward love. This is simply life unfolding all the time in front of us, asking us to grow, opening to that which makes us human, and remembering our strength and our journey.

Encouragement to remember ourselves is held in every interaction we experience. We only have to open to our hearts and choose to see life that way—as infinite opportunities flowing towards us to become and to grow into a truth and a love that supersedes all the drama involved in getting there. These opportunities come in many forms, between people interacting in every scenario of life, from road rage to making love, from a simple hello to a full-blown argument or end of a relationship. There is no end to the possibilities when it comes to the breath of how we can interact, all the levels of our communication and life together. And it's all opportunity, potential to step back and ask ourselves: What more does this interaction have to offer? What is held here for my journey toward love? Is there a gift here? Is there a deep and personal lesson to be learned? How can love present itself to my heart even now? Listening for our bigger lessons, understanding how to love ourselves rather than hold ourselves hostage to our suffering, is a journey in itself!

Jack Kornfield says, "We don't need to be so loyal to our suffering." To release ourselves from that self-inflicted loyalty to our pain, we need to look beyond all our suffering and open to the potential healing presented in every moment. In this, we become loyal to ourselves rather than our pain; loyal to our journey.

JOURNEY PROMPT

People talk about low self-esteem and feeling insecure as though it's a disease. Either you have it or you don't. But it's not that easy. These feelings exist in all of us, and at different times, we may feel more or less insecure as we relate to our world (this is true of all emotion). And it's in these moments when we realize that we're feeling insecure or less than about ourselves that we can grasp our opportunity to step back and take a good look at who we are in the moment, and perhaps how we got there. Empowered with the acknowledgment of feeling our vulnerability, we open up the opportunity to hear something within, a wisdom forgotten, that helps us remember our strength, our value and that we are really quite awesome. But first, we need to feel those moments of difficult emotion, because there's a gift that lays behind them.

All the events in our lives, gentle as well as difficult, are simply beacons contributing and guiding us to the larger messages held within our journey.

Examples of how to see life as an adventure of purpose and growth rather than a burden to be avoided:

This is one of my own little personal meditations/prayers that helps me reset and connect back into my own heart. I use some version of this regularly to keep me on track in my journey.

God, help me see this through your eyes rather than my own. Help me see this life with kindness and understanding rather than fear. Help me find a place of peace, even in my lack of understanding the ways of this world.

JOURNEY PROMPT

Build a prayer! Fill in the blanks with any words or concepts that work best for your heart, that allow you to listen and shift back toward yourself.

(Whatever you attribute universal intelligence to), **help me see this through your eyes rather than my own. Help me see this life with** *(positive desired traits of the heart)* **rather than** *(whatever emotions most separate you from your heart and truth)*. **Help me find a place of peace, even in my lack of understanding in the ways of this world.**

Now fill in your creative blanks:

(_____), help me see this through your eyes rather than my own. Help me see this life with (_____) rather than (_____). Help me find a place of peace, even in my lack of understanding in the ways of this world.

Note: Feel free to make up your own prayer/meditation from scratch. Mine is only a suggestion.

What we all need to do, and I mean everyone, is repeatedly reinforce all the fresh, new, energetic patterns of life and love that we know to be part of our hearts; to cultivate all the patterns already placed within us that only wait to be awakened and nurtured. We have to constantly feed energy to what we love in order to allow it to grow within us. Now open wide and say, ahh-love-ya.

*"Remember there's no such thing as a small act of kindness.
Every act creates a ripple with no logical end."*
-Scott Adams

A potent personal weapon I use with myself when I find that I'm wrapped up in judgment or the projection of ill will toward anyone is to find a way to wish them well. To get myself to a place where I realize I know virtually nothing about them, I'm ignorant about their lives for the most part, what has happened in the last twenty-four hours, much less the last twenty-four years, is pretty much a mystery that would probably make a big difference if I were aware of it. But I'm not. I know nothing except that they're struggling, just like all humans, and just like me, they want understanding and love.

JOURNEY PROMPT
An exercise in compassion for those you love as well as those you struggle with:
"I wish you well."

Step into your mind's eye and see that difficult someone in your mind, as though you are looking at them from afar. Then, put your hands on your heart and, as you visualize them in your mind, say to them, "I wish you well." Say it as many times as you need to. Come back to this meditation as often as you want to until your thoughts about them be-

come less charged, gentler, until you feel a shift—a shift that exudes a gentleness toward this person. This exercise can take some of the edge off of your difficult thoughts around painful encounters with others. It is an attempt to free your mind of judgment toward yourself and others, which is one way we can bring more gentleness into the world.

Try this with yourself: Using the same technique as above, envision yourself in the distance, and to the version of you that you struggle with, the one you feel challenges you, look critically at and say, "I wish you well. I wish you to be in a place that is loving and feeds your soul." Say it as many times as you wish for as long as you wish and allow the quality of that statement to sink in and manifest whatever healing and self-acceptance is needed.

Unveiling the Heart: As we move forward, deep into this spirited journey, questioning and exploring ourselves, we find ourselves examining, almost interrogating, our words and our actions to find out whether or not they've fully accessed the energy of our heart. In order to support our internal shift, we need to look again at whatever situation, pain, or struggle we've found ourselves stuck in. We have to ask ourselves: what more we can do from that sacred place of essence within, to touch the knowledge which waits beyond our thinking mind? So we ask life itself how our hearts can more fully participate in our lives, and then we wait for our sacred wisdom to move through us.

Walking with "heart" brings new passion to the question:
  If your thinking reflected your heart, who would you be?

Spend time with this question, ask yourself: *If your thinking reflected your heart, who would you be?*

- How does that open inside of you as your thoughts reflect through your heart?

- What does that look and feel like?

- Strive to answer the question: who do you become when you walk in this life with your astounding and radiant heart first?

- Are you, perhaps, once again, a little more of yourself?

This becomes the most powerful exercise in developing an internal fitness that radiates into the world. It helps **you** radiate into the world. Holding the stronger intention of living more through the heart helps us cultivate and reconnect with our heart's brilliant message of peace. When we understand the use of its vast potential, walking forward, connected to our heart, becomes an essential power statement that's always accessible for us to embrace life with. Ultimately, it energizes us to walk authentically in our truth, our love, and our personal power. It is, indeed, what we all need to embrace in order to once again become ourselves.

Soooo… Welcome to your journey; your journey back to you.

Lets take a look at all those blame arrows we've been shooting around most of our life. Aiming them at others, as well as ourselves, and how about the careless firing off of those judgments and the "you're not good enough," "I'm not good enough" attitude arrows that we've all been so well trained at using. Let's step back and take a look at them as well.

We shoot our weapons so freely, fired out of fear and the inability to see one another as real and valuable. Our arrows can be re-tipped though—a little compassion, kindness, tolerance and understanding is a good start. Then, permission from the heart before we fire, and we might find that it's not more ammunition we need, it's wisdom to know when to use it that would most serve us.

When we recalibrate all those weapons for the greater good that we can bring to this world, all that's required is true recognition of what our hunt is really about.

In self-compassion, we have to offer ourselves the same understanding and loving presence we want to bring to and receive from others. In love, we can only offer what we have for ourselves.

If we can't love ourselves, the thought of really loving anyone, truly loving someone else in a big way, is a show stopper. It can't really happen, because all-encompassing love, the love that includes you, has not yet evolved within, and so it cannot be given away. And that's quite a conundrum for the mind. It constantly loops us back to the ancient question of self-love, and the inevitable question of who we're asked to become persists within us; if we're not able to offer ourselves the gift of love and compassion, are we really able to fully offer anyone else that same gift? And then, in order to offer that gift, the most important gift we can bring to the party, who do we need to become? And then, how do we live our lives?

We need to perfect these things for ourselves—this love, compassion, understanding, and all the ideas that touch love. We need to explore all our self-love and compassion and create a presence within that opens our heart to true, pure love. We need to find love for our own very unique and wonderful creation, love for what we are and what we've been put here to be, and simultaneously open in the same way towards others.

Don't miss your opportunity to know love.

Don't miss love. It's the only thing you're really meant to latch on to. Don't miss that precious mark placed inside you, held in your heart and waiting to be released into the world. Don't miss love because you're so stuck in the illusion created by fear and apathy. That's the lack of love, its poplar opposite. Don't miss love because you're stuck in all the fear-based beliefs that life is about money or acquisitions, or sex, or fame, or success, fortune, your stunningly good looks, or any of the "deadly sins." Never forget, this life isn't about anything other than love.

When we're stuck in our heads about desire of any kind, we all tend to get distracted from our primary objective in life, and we end up forgetting to draw on the power and wisdom of our love for our strength. Being stuck in the misconceptions of fear distorts any relationship, and we can't step forward into life as we're meant to. As we become distracted away from love, our minds are never clear, and we're forever living in a fear-based world until, finally, we decide to choose again, to return to love.

Take your heart back, take back your life.

Don't miss your opportunity to remember you're love.

The goal is honest compassion. It forces you to remember. You cannot simultaneously be in compassion and judgment—judgment about yourself or judgment about others.

Just because you happen to think something, some arbitrary thought or even one you think is important, doesn't mean you have to cling to it, because attachment is voluntary. You don't have to take your thinking so seriously that you end up blowing some thought out of all proportion and end up giving away your life because you've attached to an idea that may not even have a shred of truth associated with it. We're often the ones making a thought true with our assumptions and tender feelings. We attach vital importance where it doesn't belong, and it disrupts our life. This is especially depleting when we're stuck in a world of thought that's not nearly as big as we've made it. A little hindsight goes a long way when you're honestly asking yourself, "Is that true? And how important was that, really?"

Life and love is not so much about developing the things around you as it is about incubating what's already inside of you.

So, what spirited egg are you trying to hatch?

If we want to really know what we're made of, we have to open to a world that may indeed scare us. Be open to that, because it's in embracing our vulnerability that we find our true strength, our love. It's where we find ourselves.

If your objective is to fully explore the ocean, then staying on its surface will never satisfy your craving. Just like our journey, the choice to go deeper must be presented and accepted, and that can only happen through you.

Like Rafiki said to a frustrated and depressed Simba while looking for himself in the reflection of the water hole: "No, look deeper."

"Come, seek, for search is the foundation of fortune, every success depends upon focusing the heart."
-Rumi

Oh, that moon is strong!

A commitment to a relationship is not that dissimilar to a full moon. Both a relationship with another person, especially a romantic one, and a full moon amplifies whatever energies are in its presence. If there is love, it amplifies that, and if there are emotional issues that need work or struggles that keep us from loving, it amplifies those. It's natures way of "cranking up of the sound" and bringing our attention to the things we need to work on. There's a purpose in it all. It helps us create the potential for growth. We only have to welcome it.

So the purpose of this intensification of our thinking, of turning up the volume in our minds, is to help us pay attention to our journey. It helps us clarify the things that are standing in the way of our growth, and it allows us an opportunity for deeper clarity around the issues that keep popping up and keep us in distortion and from our love. Life finds a way to put an exclamation point on whatever we need to be looking at, whatever we should be addressing with more love in order to move closer to ourselves. Be grateful for the partner who helps you remember who you are, especially when they annoy the #%!$ out of you. They're doing you a real favor, they're helping you evolve. Now pet them and say, "Niiiice partner." (Well, maybe you better leave that part out.)

Periodically, we all have a way of getting disconnected from ourselves, detached from our peace and our truth as we walk through life. We find ourselves struggling with our thinking, stuck in old spirals of toxic and painful ideas, mistrusting those we care about, caught up in false and even true assumptions about others that create anxiety for everyone, all causing a sense of distance from people we love as well as ourselves.

But our challenges always come with answers, and sometimes, the most difficult part of addressing the problem is remembering that our best solution to any challenge is an internal one. Even when someone is doing his or her best to irritate you, you choose your response, and you can choose to live your life from a place of peaceful understanding, or not. Responding is always in your court.

When we unwittingly become mired in our self-importance, our ability to reach toward the needs of one another with compassion is extinguished. That needs to be fixed, because we cannot truly serve others without love.

"It's really a wonder that I haven't dropped all my ideals, because they seem so absurd and impossible to carry out. Yet I keep them, because in spite of everything, I still believe that people are really good at heart."
-Anne Frank

Remember, choices from the heart come with the flexibility to change; they give us permission to be more fluid in our nature. Living from the heart is not a rigid thing, and when we enter the world from our heart, we also open ourselves up to finding ways to do better, ways to create more love in this life.

Never hold yourself above or below others. We're all made of the same stuff. In the realms of the heart, we're all a little clone-ish, we're all really very much the same. Our details and how we live our lives are bound to be different, but our core essence, our love, is not. In those moments when we're feeling stuck in our fear and judgment of one another and ourselves, stagnated by our self-importance and anxiety, that only creates a sense of separation between us and everyone we touch, it's remembering this core of who we are that's most important for us. Because it's all about our love—that's where our healing flows through, that's where our anxious thought is eased.

Sometimes love can feel like it's a hard thing to balance,
or that it falls apart too quickly or too easily,
and so we step back
and we build it
again,
because
this is what we are,
this is all we were really ever meant to do.

"You need not do anything.
Remain sitting at your table and listen.
You need not even listen, just wait.
You need not even wait, just learn to be quiet, still and solitary.
And the world will freely offer itself to you unmasked.
It has no choice, it will roll in ecstasy at your feet."
-Franz Kafka

We get ourselves wrapped in worry, in the opinions of others, in our learned belief systems of society, religion, politics, and simply forget that we have been blessed with creation. That in our creation exists a perfection we can only trust in. It's in that trust that life becomes abundant to us in all its gifts. This is where we see that our life was made perfect, including in its challenge, and we are, in all ways, perfectly enough when it comes to life.

Have you faced up to the self-imprisonment held within your own expectations?

Some of us are just primed to take things personally, and anything that's said to us simply puts us over the ego damn; it sets us afire. We spend our lives waiting around, primed to participate in a conversation using our ego rather than our heart.

If we're not watching ourselves in a healthy way, one-upsmanship becomes a big tool in our battle cry. We wait to find an opportunity to use our mind to make us big and the other person small, someone right (preferably us) and someone wrong. And we struggle in this war of right and wrong, because to be anything less than right and correct feels depleting and threatening to our self-image and, with a little unrestrained imagination, to our lives. So, we end up living life through ideas of the ego versus the heart, functioning from a place of self-propagated tension versus the natural flow of truth and peace.

You are already what you're seeking to reconnect with. You don't have to do, learn, become anything. It's in remembering the deep truth that resides within your heart that your reconnection unfolds. Your soul and its interface with the core of your heart are the only goals worth striving for. Everything else, all the choices you make and the thoughts you manifest in your life, stem from the integrity of that perfect connection.

Honor what's being presented.

Listen to your inner whisper,
your quiet wisdom held within
your body,
your heart,
and your mind,
as they move through you with their guidance.

Always try and break away from your habitual, patterned, and automatic reactive responses in life. We can get addicted to acting in particular ways in given situations, and all we end up getting is the reaction that we're used to getting from our world. We get what we've always gotten, while never expecting anything better. So do yourself a favor, stop looking for the response from people that you've become accustomed to receiving, the reactions you've been brainwashed into believing that you deserve, and learn to create new approaches to life that feed you and don't leave you stuck in old patterns of dysfunction. You are more and you deserve more. That's a fact worth remembering and acting on in your life, and it's up to you to do something about it. And that, my friend, is self-love.

It's a very funny thing. When I think back on an old relationship where I struggled with its ending, I realized that what I loved about it most was how *I* was able to love in the relationship, that I loved and I gave myself to it. I love how I reached toward this other person purely, as best as I could. I love that I grew despite everything, that I slowly created myself with love in order to stay. And when I chose to leave, I had to, so that I could be fully present with this love that I had evolved into, so I could honor what I had become.

> "Kids don't remember what you try to teach them.
> They remember what you are."
> -Jim Henson

Forgiving is a process, not an end. Like expanding into self-love and personal transformation, it has no definable end, but for the persistent, the path forward methodically unfolds whether you want it to or not. It's an integral part of the adventure of being fully human.

JOURNEY PROMPT

Can you think of an incident in which you would like to be forgiven for your mistakes? Imagine how that might happen. Would you need to know? Why? Can you trust the best in another to forgive in their own best time? Can you let go of the need to be forgiven by another and just forgive yourself? Take a breath.

Let's face it. Sometimes life feels like nothing more than a series of struggles, vulnerable moments, and confusing situations that can leave any of us frustrated with being human. It's part of the nature of our lives in this world.

But one of the clever little tricks of being human is that we can always choose to see our world with fresher vision, and we always have the power to start again, to see life's challenges not as immovable obstacles but as opportunities presented—opportunities for healing and growth through the stuck places we hold onto in our minds. By walking through our pain, anxiousness and feelings of vulnerability, we can come out the other side stronger than we believed we were, and, once again, ourselves.

Behind all our struggle and human drama, we innately know that something doesn't feel right and good to us, and we feel naturally compelled to search for and come back to what it is to be in our truth. And the truth is that we are lovable and beautiful. The truth is that we belong here and that we are all enough. And in truth, we are not and have never been separate from our peace or our love, because we are love. And that realization, that *we are love*, is always just one beautiful thought away from our awareness.

JOURNEY PROMPT

Sometime today, take a minute and meditate on these statements:

- I am lovable.
- I belong.
- I make a difference.
- I am enough.

As you repeat each one of these to yourself, allow their message to fill every cell of your body. Pay attention to the ones you struggle with and just stay with them, hold them lovingly, knowing that they are the truth and that they just need a little work right now.

Don't be so quick to succumb to old habits of your mind when life erupts in chaos. Look for the gift behind the experience, open to its strength and beauty on top of feeling its pain. There are lessons here. Your challenge is to present them to what's most alive in you.

JOURNEY PROMPT

Huge and life-changing questions:

What is it that's most alive in you?

Where does that aliveness exist?

What is its message?

And how would this most vital part of you receive even the most difficult lessons that come with you being alive in this miracle?

When the season is right, can you leave all the precious, spiritually transformative parts of your journey behind like a snake leaves behind their skin? Can you shed what no longer fits and allow yourself to expand into an unknown movement forward? Can you continuously open yourself up to new life, even though you know you've come so far?

It's essential for us to let go of what's old, to leave behind what previously had to be worked and transformed so that we could grow. But this has to happen in order for us to pursue another season, to move toward an even deeper spirited evolution. Let the wind take away what's old, give back that well-weathered skin of life, and allow the gift of something fresh to come—a new breath, attire more properly fit for an even deeper adventure into the love, wisdom, strength, and truth that you are.

JOURNEY PROMPT

Never let your struggle become your identity. Make it into the staircase that raises you up to who you are meant to be.

> *"We are all unique, and have our own special place in the puzzle of the universe."*
> –Rod Williams

To know our own precious value and to know that we belong in this world is a gift we give to ourselves, and then, naturally, to one another. It's a quality inherent in our existence that needs to be often remembered by our easily distracted minds. We are the ones that open up and touch that inner world, owning it in ways that belong only to us—a spark of unique spirit forged by no one but you.

The opinions of others can never tell us who we are, we go within and remember our authentic truth, we already own our deeper sense of truth. We might want to find direction form others, noticing traits in people that we want to avoid or incorporate for ourselves. Especially those we hold strong feelings of admiration or distain about. It's understandable, and they help us think about who we are, but copying them is ultimately impractical because we will always create our very own flavor of being. Let others remind you who you are, but remember, your truth is already part of you.

We're all tempted to run around trying to find our strength through false means, believing that our value exists somewhere outside of ourselves. We try to chase around the opinions of others, thinking that there's a reflection there we should be yearning for, one that we see ourselves through. But that's never the case. That reflection only shows you where you've been, not who you are.

The relentless search for that good opinion on the outside eventually distances us from our own looking glass, from seeing truth through our own soul. We only need to go within to know and validate our worth and belonging in this world, to touch who we are and how we want to live—that work is ours alone. These guidelines to identity we're all looking for are already written in our hearts, and listening to their whisper is an acquired skill. Through that we connect with within, we find out that we already own our truth and we already know that we are love. Our challenge is to claim that prize and live it. Our challenge is to walk love forward, to walk into the room of life heart first, simply because we know who we are, not because we've been told to.

In touching our own precious heart, we will know that we belong in this world simply because we've been graced with being alive in it, we've been given life! So what would that look like, how would that feel, and who would you become once you touch that gift? Herein lies your challenge, herein lies your life.

We already own our deepest truth, we already own love. It just takes one more thought for us to be it.

JOURNEY PROMPT

A flower needs no help to be what it's meant to be. It can exist and blossom in the most difficult environments, and you are no different. Often, our most personal growth requires removing the blockages to our awareness, opening to all that our love can accomplish. And this begs the question: can you open your heart to love, to who you are, like a flower opens itself to the earth?

So be grateful for the flowers,
they bring color to this world,
and you do exactly the same.

Beauty is held in being alive to the experience of your wondrous unfolding life.

I am lovable
I am valuable
I make a difference
I am enough
I am worthy
I belong

Whisper these six simple lines to yourself without reservation. Can you hold them in your heart knowing their message is already in you? It's a gentle poetry for your personal remembering—a prose meant for everyone.

These are words we're meant to speak to ourselves, to own them with a conviction that spans past our self-judgment, our pain and our fear.

I am lovable
I am valuable
I make a difference
I am enough
I am worthy
I belong

This is your gift to you, and it frees you so you can share yourself with the world.

JOURNEY PROMPT

Stretching it a little further, walking a little further, an extra shot. Give yourself the freedom to love who you are, to understand the depth of your own inspired value. What could be more precious?

"Love myself, I do. Not everything, but I love the good as well as the bad. I love my crazy lifestyle, and I love my hard discipline. I love my freedom of speech and the way my eyes get dark when I'm tired. I love that I have learned to trust people with my heart, even if it will get broken. I am proud of everything that I am and will become."
-Johnny Weir

We are all meant to move in life to fulfill the great good placed in our hearts.

JOURNEY PROMPT

"When you love yourself and others, you are looking into the face of God."
-Richard Rhem

Note: Some prompts need very little commentary. This would be one of them. Sit quietly, meditate on the great good placed in your heart. It's your journey to help that come forward. What does it take for you to allow that? What would that look like? How would it feel to allow this great part of yourself to define you? Who would you become, and how would you walk in the world with that as your focus?

Your life is abundant in unique ways nobody else has ever explored! You're a miracle, an art project extraordinaire! A creator's extravaganza! The presence of you is so profound that we've not even created the words that can express all the beauty you possess. You're ineffable in your creation.

And in all that wonder, we still need to be tolerant of all the unfinished parts of us, the yet to be completed paintings of who we are within our heart, the sculptures and creative exploits within us that yearn for expression—you need to be patient with all the projects that make you, you. The end product always reflects the love that you are, that's all you need to know.

JOURNEY PROMPT

The biggest painting, sculpture, piece of art that you can ever work on is you. You're given a universe filled with all the supplies, experiences, and lessons you could ever need to create the most amazing multimedia piece

of art. Don't let the supply store intimidate you, jump in! You have unlimited credit! There's not a dictated start time, there's no required finish time, there's just a be-fully-present-to-this-amazing-miracle time. Give yourself permission to create! Give yourself permission to trash whatever you started because you know it's just not you, and start over! Give yourself permission to never be finished with any painting, any sculpture, any creation, because "finished" doesn't belong to true art, and you, you are true, authentic, beautiful art. You just need to remember that.

Marissa Peer, author, hypnotherapist, and inspirational speaker, had a presentation on YouTube called "I'm Not Enough." She talked about helping people re-align their thinking in order to better tap into their truth, their success-oriented thought, and their self-love. Marissa explained that most of us feel *not enough* at at some level. We have our own reasons for buying into our stories of not feeling enough, although none of them really hold merit. Perhaps they came through distortions in our upbringing, or giving too much credit to the way society depicts what we "should" but can never be. Regardless of their origins, the feeling of being inadequate is an endemic condition in our culture that needs to be erased from our thinking!

The irony is, nothing could be further from the truth. We are absolutely enough, and in believing the opposite, we formed for ourselves and attached to a "less than" state of being in this, our world. Not feeling enough became the mirror that we saw ourselves through, and it colored how we saw our creation. That's a perception of thought that we need to change! Our goal has to be to come back to our honest story, to look into the polished mirror of our truth—the one that reflects all of who we are in

all our vast beauty. Here's where we all remember how we were put here: We're planted on this earth absolutely, incredibly enough in amazing ways! We are all created perfectly imperfect and completely acceptable in our imperfection. We all belong here, and no doubt we all make a difference, coming here, to this world, totally worthy of nothing less than love, love, love.

So, instead of buying into our "less than" mentalities, building our lives on the passed down, inherited common denominator of weakness that we live in and interact with one another through, we need to flip that bad habit of the mind, let go of the framework we've built in ourselves that pushes us into believing that we are not enough. Our job is to flip it right back into our truth. And the truth is: We are put here amazingly enough, and that's the story we all need to inherit. We need to buy our thinking about that! Your mind does what you tell it to, so tell it wonderful things about yourself, tell it the truth, tell it "your" truth.

I am lovable
I am valuable
I am enough
I make a difference
I am worthy
I belong

The next few pages are concepts worthy of contemplation. They will bring you through feelings and ideas about what it is to know that we're lovable, hold amazing value and worth, that we are all put here enough, and our presence in the world makes a difference, and we do, in-

deed, without question or hesitation, belong here. Go through these concepts and slowly allow yourself to become absorbed into their message. Allow yourself to remember, to know with all the fiber of your creation, that you are made of pure miracle:

So of course:

You are completely lovable
You are amazingly valuable
You are born enough
You make a difference simply in your presence
You are beyond worthy
You absolutely belong here

On enough

Life can perpetuate a wide swathe of feelings inside us, anything between and including feelings of deep unconditional value and meaning, to the soul wrenching disconnect of being stuck in agony and shame. Social networks of all kinds can promote or destroy our sense of value in overt and hidden ways. But our real value and self-love already exists within us.

We know in a deep, intuitive way that we belong here, that our spirited and creative presence makes a difference in this world. Reaching this place is the goal, but in the meantime, be kind, dole it out to others.

When we get pushed to believe in the opposite direction of our value, we're forced to seek the truth, to undo past beliefs and understand that no one can control our sense of value and acceptance but us. We end up finding the truth of what we're created as realigning with the internal love that defines us all as precious, worthy, valuable, lovable, and awe-inspired spirited human beings. We find everything we could ever want by looking within ourselves, no judgment, no *should'ves* or *could'ves*, but simply gratitude for this vast experience of being created through and being one with a love that flows forever.

> "Run like hell, my dear, from anyone likely to put a sharp knife into the sacred, tender vision of your beautiful heart."
> -Hafiz

You are enough.

"What could be more futile, more insane, than to create inner resistance to something that already is?"
-Eckhart Tolle

Your very presence has shifted the fabric of this world in a way that no one else could have. You inherently make a difference. You don't need to do anything, your presence is enough, and, in turn, you only need to remember that you are, indeed, completely enough, created completely acceptable, even in your imperfection.

> "Inner peace births world peace… that is how important you are."
> -Jyotika

The School of Love. It's the Universal Promise.

Always happy and perfect, no matter what! No matter what? Hmmm... I think we might have missed riding in that rodeo. But it's okay, because the human experience brings so much more to us than happy and perfect. These are just small parts of a much bigger journey. Our human experience brings a vast array of life, emotion, and heart-centered adventure to us, and we need to connect with it all from inside ourselves. Connect with a deep surrender to everything we're presented. We need to submerge ourselves into life, to hold our heads under its water until we realize that we're all meant to swim here, breathe here, to fly with an untethered freedom here. There's a voluntary quality to opening our eyes to our world, to being present to our journey. It makes it inevitable that we'll feel the sting of life as we struggle to focus and find our way past its difficulty and pain. After all, we're looking for more than our pain, we're opening ourselves up to moving forward, we're striving on the journey toward our natural inheritance of love, and its promise doesn't include *easy all the time*. It's work that doesn't get accomplished without a sense of purpose and determination on our part.

Always happy and perfect. Not the promise that came with life, not what we came here for. It's about growth—growth absolutely is the prize. Growth is the ticket. That's our golden ring to reach for! Our personal growth is guaranteed if we choose to participate with the program of getting the most out of life. It's through negotiating our challenges, interacting with them and learning with one another that we grow in this life. It's the perfection of creation, and this world puts us in the position

to have plenty of that growth stuff. The only caveat is we just have to choose it. And through that, we're taught what we most need to learn: the challenge of learning the depth of our love.

The un-challenged student never becomes the expert, never expands to become the best employee, most skilled craftsman, strongest athlete, or most gifted health provider, because it's the ones who work their way through the journey with tenacity and volition, the ones that hold tightly onto their purpose despite the struggles they encounter, they're the students that excel beyond anything they understood as possible. So be persistent with love, because it's in your persistence that your success unfolds.

Supplied with a plethora of imperfections, we're all running forward into life (granted, sometimes a little crazy-headed), striving to negotiate through it, and at the same time, see and live beyond our struggles and work through our mistakes and personal glitches. And even through all this, in our hearts, we all know that our ultimate desire is to know love, to find our truth despite any number of flaws in our behavior or hitches in our emotional giddy-ups. Granted, it's hard to find grace for ourselves as we stumble around on this path of being human, loving ourselves through our mistakes, while holding onto a passion for our journey through the difficult times and drama of life. And still, we choose to grow, to grow through those mistakes and challenges with the end point being that we remember we're not defined by our struggle, and when we let them, they can help point us back to ourselves. We find that, given the opportunity, our problems can lead us back to our authentic identity, and it's here we understand that the whole point of life, the reason behind this

world, is to create a place where we can search for and find the freedom of living in deep, full, and spirit-fed love. It's the perfection in the room, our personal evolution in action. Love, that's what we come here for, what this school was created for. We just have to choose to be its student.

When life feels overwhelming, remember: difficult roads, bumpy as they may be, often lead to beautiful places within.

"This is a course in miracles. It is a required course. Only the time you take it is voluntary. Free will does not mean that you can establish the curriculum. It means only that you can elect what you want to take at a given time. The course does not aim at teaching the meaning of love, for that is beyond what can be taught. It does aim, however, at removing the blocks to the awareness of love's presence, which is your natural inheritance. The opposite of love is fear, but what is all-encompassing can have no opposite.

This course can, therefore, be summed up very simply in this way:

Nothing real can be threatened.
Nothing unreal exists.
Herein lies the peace of God."

-A Course in Miracles

Just like you, I'm a human being doing my best to honor this journey.

And being human comes with the privilege and responsibility of acting stupid sometimes. A responsibility that we all take quite seriously. We make choices that ultimately have a covert purpose, which is to help us find our larger, more hearty selves. And just because we started with a stupid moment, it doesn't mean we have to live there. It doesn't require us to stay stupid, because the upside of this privileged place is that we learn, thank goodness! Besides, we have to at least try to attain and maintain *some* level of dignity in life, don't we?

The whole world is trying to get your attention, screaming your name over and over again, showing you in every way possible that you are enough. Don't make the mistake of trying to put value on the scream. It's just an attention getter. Your job is to listen to the underlying messages. Regardless of the acts, words, occurrences, the intention of life is only to wake you up to your presence in the miracle; your gift of being alive and one with that miracle.

Sometimes, when we feel so far away from believing in who we are, it's important to build a road map, a framework of sorts, back to our center.

Begin by seeing the brilliance in others, finding gratitude for their presence in this world. And after you've spent some good time cultivating a picture in your heart for those you love, put yourself there, find your own point of entry for that love. Give yourself the same honor and dignity you would bring to those you love. After all, you're part of the group, and you absolutely deserve all your love, too!

Pay attention to your presence in the light of love for you. How does our breath, confidence, and your open heart shift in this place of self-love? In becoming and knowing love for ourselves, how do you walk forward in life? Do you stride, swagger, run, dance, twirl, laugh, roll on the ground, hop, jump up and down, play, sing, hum, and shout out as you move toward your love? Ahh, don't worry about it, because as we grow, the how-to-walk-forward question pretty much answers itself, and that answer is always just perfect.

The act of reclaiming ourselves asks us to release from anything that depletes us. We need to let go of our exhausting thoughts and anxious habits, because life is asking for more than that. It's asking us to engage it, to live it with a tenacity that rejuvenates us. So engage it in a way that no matter what you're doing, you hold yourself up to the world with a reverence that asks: what's the most precious use of your time in this world now, and how will you live your life today?

Immerse yourself in your truth. The truth that lays beyond all your old and unproductive habits of the mind. Remember, you were put here as an absolute miracle, completely enough in your creation. You don't have to hide behind the drama of any stories, any ideas of suffering attached to the stubborn mind, because you, in all your love and glory, you, as a being of love, are your own best story, one worthy of attachment!

Bad choices don't define you. They're simply our bumps, our ripples in life, needing to be smoothed out with a little kind attention, and in no way will they ever undermine the fact that you belong here, and that you're both lovable and loved.

Finding peace is not a job of micromanaging your thoughts, or about thinking yourself into a perfect life. It's more about releasing your thought management techniques and recognizing the nature and quality of your thinking. Seeing thought as an abstract flow that we can choose to attach to or not, we understand that our thinking always shifts, it inevitably changes, and our job is to keep a gentle attention toward a kinder, more loving, and stronger way of being in this world—not attaching to the negative that only creates more anguish and struggle, but opening to the very thing we yearn for most, that which cultivates peace.

It's your choice. You point yourself where you want to go and simply do your best in any particular moment to open to that direction.

You choose how you think, not that you think.
So with integrity, choose your thinking. Don't let your thinking choose you.

This human journey of ours is a full contact sport!

It's the practice of creating a state of being that allows us to be more fully present in the essence of life. More present in this world and more present in our truth.

Take a breath... Allow yourself to settle into that gentler place within, the venue where you give yourself the freedom to see your own incomparable beauty. Journey forward, reconstitute all the love you've stored away. See, understand, embrace all the brilliance that is you.

TAPPING INTO YOUR *personal* PRESENCE

MINDFULNESS, PRESENCE, ESSENCE AWARENESS

"People say that what we are all seeking is a meaning for life. I think that what we're really seeking is an experience of being alive, so that our life experiences on the purely physical plane will have residence within our innermost being and reality, so that we can actually feel the rapture of being alive."
-Joseph Campbell

The dance of the words of being: presence, mindfulness, essence-awareness. Use whichever phrase you wish that helps you reflect the ideas of being in the presence of your own peace, embracing the essence of your heart, and living mindful of the miracle of your creation. The differences in the phrases are far less important than what they're trying to impart to you, which is essentially: remember, you are here now, alive in this moment, and awakened… **breathe into it.**

When we finally accept that we're creatures who are truly endowed with free will, our very next challenge is one of taking full responsibility for the quality of thought that we engage in.

Our free will is a gift offered in our creation—our very human gift, a gift held within our body, mind, and spirit that helps us generate and cultivate our health and healing, find our wellness and strength, from a place positioned within our core. The gift of free will comes with the simple requirement of requesting our attention and maintaining our intention on its presence within us and its function in our lives. We need to keep it available in our lives at levels that acknowledge its presence and accomplish this goal—one of assisting our human journey and facilitating the remembering of our truth, our power, and our love.

Free will is exactly that. It's the gift of being able to free our minds to negotiate the quality of our lives with; to work through the biological fear that we create and attach to in our thinking, and to consciously choose to participate or not in the habits of the mind. It offers us the personal freedom and potential to create new ways of thinking in any circumstance that doesn't require us to live in the old habits of the mind. Free will essentially helps us define our lives with fresh thought, thinking that can continuously guide us with love, kindness, strength, and justice.

How then do we negotiate our tendency to get stuck in the fight or flight mechanisms of the mind when we feel like someone is making our world unsafe? How do we use our free will to re-create our thinking so it matches our heart? How do we find our kindness and our justice, our love and our strength, in the midst of personal challenges? The answer to

the question might be simply to realize that our mind may be stuck in a belief system that's not true, that we're just stuck believing the thinking that we've received or created and attached to, and we need to open up to seeing things in a way that puts us into that place of wisdom, that quality of thought that reflects our strength, the understanding held within our personal truth, and a quality of thinking that incorporates kindness as well as healthy justice.

Most of our anxiety and struggles are our perceived problems—issues that we see as mistakes and imperfections that we put into the category of dysfunction or not being enough. But it's just our thinking, it's just the biological function of the brain doing what the brain does, entertaining whatever thought enters its realm. But it's just thought, and it will, given the space, naturally shift, and in a good way, especially if we maintain our intention on the strength and wisdom of the heart. And you either pay attention to that place within you or you don't. That's the choice, that's where our free will comes into play.

And that's the truth of it, that's what we all need to remember, because our free will is meant to be used in conjunction with the heart, not with our fear.

And that begs the question: when you're in fear, is free will even available to you, or do you have to connect with the essence of the heart in order to retrieve solutions that are a reflection of your truth, answers that are really already within you? The answer seems to be held within the question. Fear comes through the outside, and, at the core of our creation, it isn't what we were created with. In essence, fear exists in the

absence of love and, therefore, it's not of our authentic identity. We only come here with the ability to recognize it and negotiate it. It does not exist in the core of what we are.

It's important for us to get past our propensity to judge ourselves or one another through the mind of the ego and self-importance, hubris and deprecation, or any of the seven deadly sins (pride, greed, lust, envy, gluttony, wrath, and sloth). All these judgments and lower consciousness energies simply keep us away from peace and serve well to distract us into lingering in their presence. Subsequently, we can end up festering in their waste products. Not a pretty sight.

Story:

Free will comes with responsibility. Once you realize that you have free thought, and you can think or do whatever you choose. That knowledge puts you in the driver's seat of your life. Because once you except that challenge, you're asked to hold it with responsibility, and your life becomes yours. The choices of living through the old patterns and paradigms of thinking that once dictated the quality of your life experience now need to be re-evaluated. Free will choice dictates a certain level of knowledge that you're making the choices that are defining your life. And it's from this place that we're asked, once again, to walk forward, to present our authentic identity to the world as best we can.

I had a patient who was concerned about their hip. Apparently, their partner would only allow them one particular position during intercourse, and that position hurt them. It was pretty evident that nobody was happy with the outcome. This created resentment between the two, and

it was very evident the issue being discussed created concern for the quality of the relationship as well as its potential for a future. They couldn't see past this restriction and, in turn, ended up restricting themselves in their thinking in the relationship. The capacity for compassion, healthy communication, or love was superseded by the old patterns of not feeling enough, being disrespected, and not getting exactly what was wanted. They were stuck in the "I, me, and mine" syndrome, only able to think about their own concerns and unable to reach towards others with a kind heart.

So, I asked them some questions. I asked them to ask themselves internally, *"How can I see this situation differently? How can I balance the fear I am feeling right now about this relationship with love and patience? How can I balance my need and my expanded self-importance with understanding and kind justice?"* And I asked them to realize and tell themselves that they have free will thought. They needed to open themselves up and be willing to look in a direction other than fear to approach this problem with. They needed to open their hearts and get out of their heads about their problem, and be willing to explore it with love rather than fear.

They did their homework, and eventually their problem was resolved with healthy communication, understanding, and patience from both. Free will ruled the day, and fear was recognized, duct taped, and put in the way-back-seat of a 1969 Buick Skylark Sport Wagon. *(Absolutely no relationship to any childhood memories associated with the author of this book!)*

It's in the acknowledgment of our free will that we're faced with the challenge and the responsibility of being the ones who make our choices. We can no longer blame others for what we decide, how we live our lives, and what we do. There's a freedom in that finally our life becomes our own, an adventure to immerse ourselves in, and it really is all ours for the taking.

Affirmation: I have free will thought, and I'm willing to look in a direction other than fear and inflexible thinking to approach my challenges with. I'm willing to open to and do my best to listen to my heart, get out of my head about my struggle, and be willing to explore my issues in life with the strength of love rather than the distraction of fear.

"When you arise in the morning, think of what a precious privilege it is to be alive—to breathe, to think, to enjoy, to love."
-Marcus Aurelius

Quiet time with integrity. We rarely give ourselves the space we need in life to be soft, to be quiet, to the point of experiencing a deep quality of peace that seems rather unavailable in our self-imposed busyness. Finding our moment is hard enough, much less creating a stance within ourselves that we can hold our life with. The act of being in life with an internal stance, an importance that honors our quiet, our still point, our silence, helps us cultivate a presence that is so true to our heart that once we experience it, we change, we can no longer walk as we did, in the busy worry of accomplishment and urgency. Suddenly, we become something closer to ourselves, our smile becomes softer, our mind simpler, and we know we will not enter the world in the same way that we did previously.

There is an integrity to the quiet in my heart. Giving my life to the distractions of the world is unnecessary. So often in life, "this can wait" is my best answer to the frenzy that abounds. Life, in all its excitement, begs to take me away from my center. I simply want to smile at it and say, "I am breath, I am peace. I am open to the life held within this quiet moment."

Once in a while, we could all use a little cataract surgery!

Opening to life's aliveness, present to its breath, knowing the great awareness of our miracle, we make the choice to manifest an awareness, a way of being that we could never have known earlier. It's a courageously deep, full, and vital expanse into our own world. We see what we could not see, explore what was previously missed, and touch others in ways of the heart we avoided. Being a living presence opens us up. Ideas and thoughts we've often rejected are now possible and vibrant within us. The cataracts are removed, and we can't stop looking at all the beautiful colors of life. Having stepped beyond the clouds, we can see again, and we walk through the lush botanical garden of our life present and absorbed in being here.

This is how life works: We pop open and notice our more-ness in the world—more present, more alive, more ourselves, more spirit, more love, more coffee (that's mine) in your life. We see more of the spark that makes us real, see deeper into the people around us, reach out more, and consciously extend ourselves into a new, fresh world every day. The word "abundance" finally finds its meaning; it's understood and defined through the heart, and we realize that we're smack dab in the middle of it. A life that was overlooked is attended to, a quality of thought previously asleep to is awoken within us. We remember something of what we're meant to be.

Looking beyond this whirling world, beyond all our dead and frantic thoughts and fears, we free ourselves from the addiction to control

our way through life. We don't take our thinking so seriously, and avoid indulging in all the anxious questioning that we drag ourselves through with every living choice we make. We release ourselves to the whispers of the heart, seeing that right and wrong is not always set in stone, but can be limiting and questionable in its nature. Stepping past the potential traps of good and bad, right and wrong, we look beyond the self-imposed stop and go's of life and we free ourselves from the beliefs that block life. We engage with the knowledge and wisdom placed not in our brain, but in our heart.

Our presence to this life enables us to open to a love and aliveness within that holds no expectation of how things should be, no boundaries over what we're allowed to feel or not feel, and allows us to be present in all that we have missed because we've been so distracted by a world that keeps us looking elsewhere for life.

There are moments in life that define your story beyond what you believe your life to be. Pay attention. These are your moments of opportunity—the doors opening that return you to your heart.

JOURNEY PROMPT

I think this is a kind of tough entry to get through. It asks you to identify and explore those deep and unpredictable moments that have helped shape the heart of you. For quite a while, I thought about the many moments in my life, big and small, that catapulted me past perceiving my world as ordinary and perhaps bland or, in other words, taking it for granted. It's as if these transforming events were put in front of me to say, "Hey! Pay attention! There's more to your life than you can ever believe! Listen up, take a look!"

Here is an example of one of my "moments." It might help you explore your own better, but don't limit yourself to this. Your moments are preciously yours. Let them unfold and come forward in their own unique way.

Midway through a meditation retreat with Jon Kabat-Zinn and Saki Santorelli, I realized I was stuck in cement, thinking cement. Now, I'd been here before. I just never went so deep. I was in insecure, paranoid, self-deprecating, and depressed—all around a relationship that I thought defined me. I knew this place well, but it felt bigger, more relentless, and more electrified than it had ever felt before. It was a full-blown thought attack, and I felt paralyzed in it.

I felt stuck most of that day and the prior day, but, at one point, I realized that I was giving up my one precious life to this disruptive, life-sucking thinking. The phrase that came to me and changed the quality of how I would live my life was: **what thought is worth giving over your life to?** And the obvious answer is: *none of them.* Why would you trade your precious life for time spent in disruptive thought? That little moment defined me beyond anything I previously believed could, and continues to.

The objective of being on a journey is to cultivate a way of life where you can fully enjoy and live in your moments rather than be distracted and consumed by them!

JOURNEY PROMPT

Consider the moments when consuming thoughts of the mind have robbed you of your a heart-centered life—anxious thinking, disruptive assumptions, judgments and needy ideas, thinking that doesn't serve your spirit or your heart. (No need to make a list. It's better to let those distortions of the mind settle away anyway.)

Moments of joy? (Make a big list and find ways to add to it!)
1.

2.

3.

Sufi mystics (order of Mevlevi dervishes) incorporate the practice of whirling to help solidify their relationship with God.

Broadly defined, whirling is *the art of finding the unmoving center of your being as life moves and whirls around you. Sought through focusing on God, and spinning one's body in repetitive circles, arms are open. The right arm is directed to the sky to receive God's grace, the left hand, where the eyes are fastened, is turned toward connecting to this earth. The intention held while one whirls is to embrace all humanity with love.*

For most of us, the act of whirling like a dervish is a symbol, an example, of the holding of intention to maintain ourselves in a heart-centered life directed by love while our busy world speeds past, trying to mindlessly pull us along. In our strength, our center, we maintain ourselves in that solid place of heart while simultaneously doing our best to take care of what needs to be dealt with in life. There's a balance to it all. This is an art of the heart, and we could all benefit from practicing it. Holding the intention comes first. Spinning in a circle—well, that's optional, although you never know what you might get from whirling until you try! Embracing all humanity with love is a worthy endeavor, but do yourself a favor and practice in a soft place with no sharp corners!

JOURNEY PROMPT

This is where our Power Statements come in handy. They can help us reboot, put ourselves back on center, back in our truth when we get overwhelmed with the chaos around us. They can help us see that we can be in the chaos but we don't have to become the chaos. So, come on, keep adding to that list!

How strong anything becomes depends upon how well you feed it—plants, animals, relationships, integrity, gratitude, and all thought, all depend on nurturing to flourish. So, pay attention to what you're feeding, because that's always what grows, especially in your mind.

JOURNEY PROMPT

In the morning, as you're getting ready for the day, pause for a moment to ask yourself what strength you want to reinforce in your life today. Have a phrase or mantra you can hold through the day that answers the questions: What am I going to feed my mind today? What state of being will I reinforce within myself today?

It might simply be holding onto a word or phrase like gratitude, trust, allow, kindness, non-anger, integrity, self-worth, forgiveness, or you could wrap a bigger story around it that guides you towards your best self, like remembering a compliment, or the moral of a story you read earlier. Essentially, it's anything that helps you remember your truth, anything that can easily be accessed that helps you stay in your honor and power, or helps you know your better way of being in this world.

JOURNEY PROMPT
A quick little exercise:

Write down a couple words that represent qualities you would like to embrace. These can be your **default words**—the words you always go back to for grounding into your truth and strength, the ones you can easily grab on the run!

My default power word list:

-
-
-
-
-
-

*"I am only one, but still, I am one. I cannot do everything,
but still, I can do something; and because I cannot do everything,
I will not refuse to do something that I can do."*
-Edward Everett Hale

We're all continuously trying to answer the question: **what is the most precious use of my time in this moment?** And we're always looking for our most right answer to that question. It's a confusing game we play inside our heads—rationalizing, avoiding, and being confrontational with all the thoughts that pull us toward or away from love. Ideally, the most precious use of our time requires us to examine whether we are lovingly considering our own highest good or the highest good of others.

It can be a difficult question to negotiate, this precious use of time. Clear answers are often hard to discern, however, when we keep ourselves and our thoughts directed through a rational integrity, one based in good, it refines our choices, and we can opt for what benefits our world most. We can make our best choice.

JOURNEY PROMPT

How do we travel on this journey of the heart without imploding into the world's busyness? How do we live our lives and embody love amongst all the mind's chatter? Pay attention to your answers. You might get lucky, because they might know where peace resides.

A curiosity about meditation is that it slows you down, and within that, it helps you notice more of what's happening in your life. You step back from your fast-moving world, and shocked at yourself, you notice how intensely your life is moving. It might look a little crazy-making to you, and when you look a little closer, suddenly, you see how you've been participating in and contributing to the problem, willingly and enthusiastically. As a matter of fact, you see that it's you supplying life with its quadruple espresso shots of stress and tension, regularly! You're your own pusher!

So slow down, and breathe more deeply into life. This is where you familiarize yourself with the term *mindfulness!* You've been driving ninety-five miles an hour on a road meant to be a scenic route, and you've missed way more of life than you're ever going to begin to see if you keep driving so fast on a road that was meant to be enjoyed. And then, of course, there are always going to be tickets to pay! You never think of those, but they're inevitable, and they often get paid by some of your most vital organs!

Life is an abundant experience, and we're meant to be in it. Quieting the mind actually helps you move more fully into your experience. It's such an irony: as you slow down, your life automatically fills up, and you literally experience more of it. It's an amazing bargain in a very meaningful way.

JOURNEY PROMPT

Consider what you can do differently or even eliminate in your life that might potentially help you reclaim some quiet space, some peace, or simply some much needed time in your life to devote to the projects of the heart that hold more life for you. It's so easy to get wrapped up in the treadmill of life, feeling like you're constantly enveloped in a competition where whoever can do the most, go the farthest, visit the most places wins! But step back periodically through the day, especially when you feel stressed, and consciously look at all the unnecessary stressors of life. All the distractions to life that we can absolutely re-frame for ourselves. Pay attention to the things that feed that little monster inside of you that fills your head with the idea that we are here to do, do, do, and accomplish, and conquer, and peace can wait. Well, I'm here to tell you, peace is more important than do, do, do. So open to some new thought, some heart-centered living, and re-set what looks so important to the mind; let the heart have a word or two.

> *"Every moment is enormous and it is all we have.
> Our life is a path of learning to wake up before we die."*
> -Natalie Goldberg in Long, Quiet Highway

Can you become comfortable with your own quiet?

Sometimes, as we meditate, we get a little taste, a momentary glimpse, of a calmer place within—a state of being that's vaguely familiar to us and, at the same time, we also know it completely. Our breath relaxes and, for a moment, we're comfortable with our own quiet as our mental world relaxes. For one brief moment, our mind is congruent with that gentle, peaceful place which always exists within us. Be grateful for these gifts, and allow the taste to accumulate until quiet's presence remains in a strong, steady, life-enhancing way.

JOURNEY PROMPT

Consider three ways that you can touch, even for the briefest of moments, that quiet place within—at home, during time with friends, even in the chaos of work.

How would you describe your process of finding quiet? It's okay if the question confuses you. Sometimes, the best first step is simply opening up to the possibilities and ideas the question presents.

1.

2.

3.

Tools for Quieting the Mind

Mantras and meditations are tools that can help guide us into a quieter mind. They can help us reset our attention, helping us turn down the volume of our head chatter, sometimes facilitating a tiny shift, and other times pulling us away from the churning of insistent thinking that can drive us a little batty.

There are a variety of approaches we can take, and many approaches can work: hiking in the woods, cleaning the house, sitting quietly, singing a favorite line of a song. It's a personal preference, and you have to find your own best practice. The only goal is to find a way to ease our thinking minds so that peace can have a chance to be in our lives.

Our goal:
- To allow our minds to open to a calmer way.

- Create an environment of internal healing, emotionally, spiritually, and physically.

- Make space in our lives so we might hear the faint, beautiful whisper of our heart.

Mantra

For the purposes of this entry, a mantra is a valued word, phrase, or sound that carries an almost sacred meaning to you. It can be repeated in the mind or verbally as many or few times as you would like. My advice is for

you to listen for the simple words or phrases that your heart would have you speak.

I commonly use the phrase, "I wish you well." I say it to individuals as well as the world at large. And I often simply use the words, "Thank you," or, "Gratitude," as a general, very grateful way to open to all that this world brings to my life.

Meditation

And again, for our purposes in this entry, we will lean on Jon Kabat-Zinn's description of the goal of mindfulness meditation, which is to be quietly present to each moment of our experience—a common goal in many meditations.

> *"Mindfulness means moment-to-moment, non-judgmental awareness. It is cultivated by refining our capacity to pay attention, intentionally, in the present moment, and then sustaining that attention over time as best we can. In the process, we become more in touch with our life as it is unfolding."*
> *–Jon Kabat-Zinn*

> *"Meditation is not a way of making your mind quiet. It's a way of entering into the quiet that's already there–buried under the 50,000 thoughts the average person thinks every day."*
> *–Deepak Chopra*

> *"With mindfulness, you can establish yourself in the present in order to touch the wonders of life that are available in that moment."*
> *–Thich Nhat Hanh*

JOURNEY PROMPT

There are so many teachers and techniques available to us these days. Explore what forms of meditation best suit you. Then, it's just a matter of spending time with your practice of choice and practicing (often the hardest part). But it's all for the best reason. It's for you, for your peace, and it's for your heart.

"I went to the woods because I wished to live deliberately, to front only the essential facts of life, and see if I could not learn what it had to teach, and not, when I came to die, discover that I had not lived."
-Henry David Thoreau

One moment, one breath, even half of a breath of mindfully quiet time can lead you into your gentleness, your inspired wisdom. It can help open your mind to fresh solutions around life's problems, cultivate inner peace, and help you grasp onto deeper thoughts of forgiveness. You have to choose to step toward that grounding place, that internal mecca always accessible to you. Your breath puts it a little more within your reach, it moves you a little closer to recognizing and remembering your truth.

Just this little touch of breath, this caress of your own soul, sparks the knowledge of something sacred and alive within. The act of walking in this world in a breath-full way is far more authentic to your true nature than anything you can create with your over-thinking, anxious mind. So, take a beautiful breath and remember your heart.

JOURNEY PROMPT MEDITATION

- Find a comfortable, quiet place to sit. A seat where you can keep your back a little straighter and your posture a little bit more upright.

- Sit for a minute and calm your breath to a pace that's a bit deeper and a little slower than usual.

- Now, if possible, put your right hand over your heart and your left hand on your stomach, or just keep your attention on these areas as you continue to breathe. There shouldn't be too much movement of your heart hand, and your stomach hand should be slowly moving in with your inhalations and out with your exhalation.

- As you breathe, imagine your heart filling with breath every time you inhale, as though you're breathing into your heart.

- Sit in this position and with this breathing technique for a couple of minutes.

- After you've established a bit of body memory with your breathing, allow your mind to entertain feelings of gratitude and appreciation. Hold on to these feelings and apply them to every part of your life as best you can. Create stories around them if you need to. Gratitude and appreciation can be applied everywhere at some level.

Be creative. There are many other words of wellbeing that can be applied to this technique, like honor, kindness, open-heartedness, compassion, love, gentleness, generosity, wisdom, peace, and self-love to name a few. And you can apply any of your phrases and Power Statements as well. Just have fun and strive for a bigger, stronger heart.

What is your meditation emoji?

Meditation: The intentional act of cultivating an acute, profound awareness of your personal presence in your life—an awareness that points you toward gratitude for this miracle of being alive, regardless of any other acquired belief system.

JOURNEY PROMPT

There are many definitions and descriptions surrounding meditation. And there are multiple approaches to explore, but the most important part of your search is to find out what works for you, to find what best helps you find peace.

This is about *your* peace, a peace that allows you to remember who you are, and helps you sit with it with a big smile on your face. That's the point of it all: to create your own internal, peaceful smile. Your own personal emoji.

Breathe—Your—Self.

"Within you, there is a stillness and a sanctuary to which you can retreat at any time and be yourself."
 -Hermann Hesse

Meditate on how you see yourself in five, ten, or twenty years. Explore potential personal accomplishments, health goals, and who you would like to become. People who explore their future selves in meditation tend to make more responsible choices in their present world; choices that orient them toward the direction of their inspiration.

JOURNEY PROMPT

Here's a thought: if you're x-years old and you want to be healthy, happy, and more deeply inspired in five, ten, or even twenty years, spend time in your meditation seeing that person you know already exists in you.

What choices might you naturally make as you walk toward the future you? What choices would they make on your behalf? What can help you evolve and form your deepest truth over time? (Yes, even though we only have this moment! Humor me here a for a minute!) Do any of the concepts you've come across in this book or any other help guide you towards your happier and healthier +20 vision? What about diet or lifestyle choices? Anything that a current and future you might see as valuable to the journey?

Meditating with gratitude toward your beautiful life and seeing your world with appreciation creates movement in that direction. Use that to your benefit and for the benefit of all those around you.

In guided meditation, we're often asked to pay attention to the breath, and whoever's leading the class might go on to explain how each breath brings forward life, and with it, our next moment. They might even go on to explain how breathing keeps us all connected to the earth, connected to one another, and rooted in a deep awareness of being alive to ourselves.

Breathing is one of those catalysts that helps highlight our human experience. Pay attention to it, allow the breath to flow throughout the body. It can inspire an awareness of being alive not previously touched by us. We breathe not only because we need oxygen to survive, but because we need the continuous reminder that we're immersed in this world in a living and brilliantly alive way. Paying attention to our breath reminds us to pay attention to life itself. It's as though each breath sets us up to be aware and present to the miracle of being. So stay open to all possibilities held within your body. The universe doesn't ask for much, only your willing immersion in it.

JOURNEY PROMPT

Experiment with yourself. Try breathing into your heart or any particular area of the body that you'd like to bring a little lovin' to, pay attention to for healing, or simply to experience the full presence of it.

As you breathe, see how your awareness of that organ, system, or area shifts. Does it feel different as you hold it in your mind? It has to. You're bringing thinking to it in a very conscious way. You may or may not feel it, but you're shifting and enlivening the very dynamics of your mind as it relates to your body.

The possibilities are endless, you may suddenly see yourself differently, fresh, in a new and never experienced before way. Think about it: never have you had a moment like you have right now, and never have you been in this moment, exploring what you are. It's all new, all never exactly like this, so let yourself be with it. This moment, this breath, brings new qualities of life never before encountered. Now pay attention, see what gifts evolve through you. You might feel very little, you might feel an opening up, a freeing up of the flow of energy that circulates through you. You might have a thought that seems very silly, or one that changes your life. So open up and allow that fresh experience to fill you.

All of us, yes, we're all human,
all sitting here amazed, together,
communing, bantering and laughing,
crying, complaining and arguing
having our breakfast, drinking our
beer, nibbling our treats,
and sipping our tea,
making our work, having our families,
playing our games, and feeling our thoughts.

So full of ourselves,
feeling as though we're so aware,
believing we're touching all that exists,
that we know all that potential wisdom,
laughing,
exclaiming,
announcing to the universe
that we are so profound!
We have life all figured out!
As we tend to do, pretend to know,
and we giggle at ourselves,
entertained by our own antics,

And in an unexpected nanosecond,
we find ourselves pausing, between breaths,
stepping back, remembering that, yes,
we really are simply this human heart.

JOURNEY PROMPT

There are moments when we get a tad obsessive and caught up in ourselves, stuck in our egos, wrapped up in our life and self-adoration. And in the very next moment, we're flung back to a level of conscious awareness where we can again see ourselves simply as human hearts, simply as love. We find that place of understanding where we know we're not required to do anything spectacular; that we, in our essence, are simply an expanding spirited love with a body attached.

Meditate on that for a moment. What would that look like, how would it feel, and who would you become in that moment of realization when you understand that you are a walking heart, when you understand the abundant love that exists within you?

Power Statements

In previous books, we've discussed Power Statements. The words, phrases or quotes, the stories, memories, and fables that we find ourselves relating to best—the phrases that spark our hearts. Our Power Statements act as reminders that help remember ourselves and reconnect with our personal strength. Through them, we find inner ease, and rekindle our deeper truth and identity. They're the words and concepts that we hold that remind us of our authentic selves.

Power Statements always appear around us. They're the ideas and understandings just waiting to be recognized and integrated into our lives, hidden in a line in a movie or in a book, in the pages of a magazine, or even on billboards. We hear them through a quote in a sermon at church, or maybe in a passing comment from a friend or even a stranger. The point is, when it has resonance with your truth, take note! Write it down! Remember the energy behind it, because it's yours to hold as long as you need it.

Power Statements act as an antidote to the self-talk that creates fear and weakness within us. They remind us that we are not our negative or unproductive thinking, and Power Statements help put us back on track in life, pointing us down a path that inspires and rejuvenates rather than depletes.

JOURNEY PROMPT

What would it look like, what would it feel like, and who would you be if your thinking matched your heart? This might be the most valid question you can ask yourself, the perfect question that actually helps draw you back toward your truth. **So really, again: what does it actually look like when your thoughts follow your heart? Are there feelings associated with it? And who do you become when that happens?**

Answer this and you'll see that this is where your Power Statements take shape. In your walking world, you'll naturally come across phrases and words that draw you into the heart of who you are, and therein lays the discovery of your Power Statements—those expressions that help you remember your deepest truths and provide a strength to your life that can only be brought forward through the brilliance of the word.

Creating a gentle, internal state of mindfulness is not so much about just quieting your mind—the mind is prone to chatter. More often than not, it's more about prioritizing which part of the mind you're going to give your attention to. In making space for our intuition to be heard, we naturally put the chatter of the ego and self-importance in the background, not the forefront of our thinking.

Intuition is always present for us. It's always waiting for our attention and crossing its fingers that fear is not mistaken for truth or love. So, as you're listening for that intuitive whisper, learn the difference between a breath taken with peace and one taken with tension and fear. Each, in their own way, has a message. One points out that you're on track, the other that you're stuck somewhere.

JOURNEY PROMPT

What is the useless chatter that distracts you most from hearing the whispers of your intuitive nature, hearing the language of the heart?

Here is my list of some useless thinking I've found myself getting stuck in; internal dialogue that would be best, for everyone, if I set it to the side.

1.

2.

3.

*"You can become blind by seeing each day as a similar one.
Each day is a different one, each day brings a miracle of its own.
It's just a matter of paying attention to the miracle."*
−Paulo Coelho

Question your life.

In our quest for peace, one of the most important steps that we can take in our minds is to question and quiet the authority that fear might hold in our lives. Although this is not always the case, questioning ourselves should always be an open option in our lives.

In honestly becoming more aware of our personal process, in asking the questions that help us evaluate how we're holding life, we can more effectively participate in our journey and embody a deeper sense of responsibility for our personal wellbeing and state of mind.

JOURNEY PROMPT

So the next time someone asks you, "How are you doing?" well, you don't have to give them your entire big story, but it is okay to go there with yourself. When you find some quiet time, ask yourself, "How are you doing?" and then reflect on the honest answer. Your answer, no matter what, is okay. You're strong. Open to your answer, your heart, and allow the listening ear of compassion to click in. Welcome an authentic response.

"I've never seen any life transformation that doesn't begin with the person in question finally getting tired of their own bullshit."
−Elizabeth Gilbert

As your life journey moves forward, explore all the lessons of truth, love, compassion, and awakening that you can find! Explore it all: the techniques, readings, practices, lifestyles that want to help you to know a bigger picture of love. Educate your heart, openly meet your experience, and stay present to the vast array of spirited ideas that await your journey. It's up to you to help create and embrace every opportunity for love's presence, so allow yourself to be taken by this life!

And Explore!

Practice the art of the walking meditation. As you walk, practice planting each step on the earth, floor, pavement, with great intention. As you do this, visualize leaving behind a contagious footprint of love everywhere you go, so if someone else were to touch that same spot they might feel your energetic message. Consciously take each step, paying attention so that the presence of your step marks the earth. Leave behind a legacy of love every time you touch the earth.

You can also do the same with a handshake. In the handshake meditation, linger for that extra moment while you empower your partner with a small, imperceptible, but fragrant blast of love. And for those you know in a closer, more intimate way, you can try a shoulder rub meditation, a hug meditation, or a quick glance meditation. They can all be part of your practice of planting love everywhere you go, with everything and everyone you see and touch. It's you doing your part to purify this world with truth.

"Life is a great and wondrous mystery, and the only thing we know that we have for sure is what is right here, right now. Don't miss it."
-Leo Buscaglia

I have heard that some indigenous cultures believe that everything exists in the present moment or the un-manifest moments yet to be. There's a wisdom to adopting this kind of paradigm, as it virtually eliminates our ideas of a future and a past, and it gives us permission and a kind of tool to move past the uselessness of future fear and past regrets.

Check yourself before you wreck yourself!

When our need to be seen as special *(respected, looked up to, good looking, important, brilliant, sexy, strong, wise…)* supersedes our ability to sit quietly with ourselves and be with the truths this world presents to us and through us, we blind ourselves to the real beauty of living in our precious lives.

Funny story: I was sitting at our local Starbucks, waiting to be served and feeling a little ignored by the two baristas while they were busy serving the drive-through. I was anxious to start working on a manuscript I was a little obsessive with and felt perturbed at being made to wait. As I looked at the busy fellows, I caught the eye of one of them and said, "Let me know when you're ready," and I sat down to write.

Above is the entry I started editing. It hit me like a brick, and I thought, "Damn!" smiled at myself, and resumed my writing and my waiting with a fresh, less narcissistic attitude. What an immediate lesson, no waiting there! And I find myself more open to all that life presents in the moment.

See… it might take a while, and a kick in the head,
but I pay attention!

It's a trick and a lot of personal work to pay attention to the energy we're walking in the world with. Acknowledging all the conscious and subconscious qualities that keep us looking for balance in our lives. It takes a high degree of self-awareness to recognize when we're emotionally off center, really torqued, tweaked, not walking the golden path, chasing stories, not on our best wellbeing game. But until we see it, until we feel our disconnect from ourselves, we have very little chance of opening up enough to heal it.

It takes a strong leap of faith and personal volition to walk the path of self-evaluation and self-knowledge. Those internal flashing lights that indicate being off the mark can show up subtly. You notice that you're veering off to places in your mind towards the unhealthy highway in your head. And so you learn to carefully listen to the quiet whispers that say, "Slow that freight train down, buddy. It's time to re-boot whatever program you're stuck in right now! Take a breath, come back to yourself."

So, when you feel the uncomfortable habits of the mind bubbling around in your thinking, surfacing because you've mistakenly taken a wrong turn off your better path, step back, pay attention, and acknowledge where you're at. Look at your perceptions, your feelings of being attacked, taken for granted, hurt in any way or sense of betrayal, and be quiet with your higher self for a moment. Find the understanding inside yourself that lets you see that there's always a better, less anxious way to be with what's happening. To listen for the whisper, you have to quiet the drumming of the mind.

When life presents its challenges, understand that everyone, including yourself, is doing the best that they can in that moment, given the life they've experienced so far. Be understanding about the emotional-mental space that you and those around you may have dropped into, gotten stuck in, or unintentionally bought into, and then open up to whatever it takes to settle into your personal better way of being.

It's our nature to review the events and memories of our lives. We're made to be thinking creatures, and we naturally and automatically revisit and explore what we've experienced. Memories have a way of making an appearance in our minds—sometimes its a choice, we just want to give it some thought, sometimes it happens without any help from us, the visit is somehow generated through a subconscious influence, like an unannounced dinner guest is giving us the opportunity to expand. We need to ask ourselves what we want to do with this visitor: how should we be with and see this memory now?

So when old memories visit, give yourself the opportunity and the permission to start fresh with all your thinking, all your memories. Begin again and allow yourself to see things in a new way, with more compassion, consciously looking to lovingly understand yourself and everyone in your world, forgive yourself as well as others for all the flaws that we're all negotiating, and remember to respect your life and to honor your love.

When old memories get activated, don't hold them too tight, and don't chew on them too long. Set them aside in a neutral way and invite your best self forward, then be patient.

JOURNEY PROMPT

When you find yourself stuck in an old pattern of thought, no matter what it is, give yourself a break. Say to yourself:

"Of course you would have felt what appeared to be an arbitrary emotion in *that* particular situation. It totally makes sense when you understand the nature of the mind in difficult situations. I can't imagine that anyone wouldn't have felt the same way."

Attachments to the past are inevitable, but they do serve a purpose. They allow us to create space for healing—healing and growth for ourselves and others—and then we can allow them to transform into a more neutral state and settle away.

Can you wander in your mind and open to an understanding that perhaps what's in front of all of us right now has manifested through the breath of guidance and wisdom? And though we may not have the capacity to grasp it, we only need to accept its truth. Our moments, whether difficult or beautiful, are a piece of a bigger, more infinite puzzle than we may ever comprehend. Be patient here, be kind with one another. That's always our next best choice.

"There is a voice that doesn't use words. Listen."
-Jalal ad-Din Rumi

We can get stuck in all kinds of indecision about the best way for us to move forward in life. Sometimes we just don't know what to do or which path to follow.

Step back, take a moment, question yourself: what is the most precious use of my time right now?

And then, listen for an answer. Is there a better way, a new direction? Follow where the energy of your life points you.

I had a friend who used to say, "Don't waste the calories, eat the good chocolate." That was her way of following the energy.

So, "Don't waste today's breath, do your best to be present in the miracle of your life."

The best use of my time is not spent in chasing fear. There's absolutely no peace in that. The best, most precious use of my time is being fully present to my life. "Don't waste the calories, eat the good chocolate."

Any one of us, at any moment, is always one thought from peace or fear—from being a Gandhi or thinking like a Hitler. It's our free will thought, the quality of thinking we give life to, and the level of consciousness that we cultivate within—this is what allows or prevents everything we become in this life.

What would it look like if you were in charge of the quality of thought allowed to exist in this world? If you were made the "Thought Czar" or "Thought Emperor" of this world, and you were the only one who determined what kind of thinking we all attached to and entertained? How would you work that, what rules and guidelines would you make for us all?

Can you see yourself having the power, awareness, and ability to recognize and sort through all the outside influences, the subconscious judgments, and fears seeking all of our attention? Can you see the distraction that everyone can get misdirected by through having a victim mentality? What kind of life might that create for us when we're all allowed to choose that quality of thinking in our life experience? But if you're in charge, we don't have to worry about it anymore. So tell me honorable Thought Emperor, how do we negotiate our world? How do we maintain quality of thought in this place? And good luck, you have quite the job ahead of you!

Okay! Obviously, you can't do this for everyone. It can't be and never could be a job given to anyone else, so it's a darn good thing that you're only in charge of doing it for you. So you can't control *the* world, but can control *your* world, at least as far as choosing what thinking you attach to. Now what are you going to do? How are you going to work with that? And within that… welcome to your journey.

We may not always have the answers to creating perfect thinking, but we have a pretty good idea when we're stuck and indulging in our negativity. Knowing and acknowledging that stuckness is the first great step in moving toward something better, and after that comes the courage to imagine something new, something different. So listen, listen to life with your heart, and be your own Thought Czar!

Our lives take on the energy of our thinking. And our thinking, guided by the broad sweep of either love or fear, determines our actions. The bottom line being, the quality of what we choose to think is responsible for directing how we live in this world. We always need to ask ourselves if our thinking and our actions are seeded from the heart. If so, the way we live our lives will reflect that, and the consequences of living through the heart will always be the welcome consequences of peace and love.

When we function through our heart, it transforms every thought, action, and desire of our walking journey.

JOURNEY PROMPT

In order to move closer to what is most sacred within me, what do I need to do in my life? What should I let go of and what can I include?

Let's all agree to try not to give into our urge to follow our old familiar ways of unproductive thinking.

How about trying this: We all agree to make courageous attempts to recognize when we're stuck in our disruptive urges and stubborn or negative qualities of thought. We take the time to clearly define what our disruptions are and acknowledge how they limit our ability to be more fully present and loving in our lives. Then, we agree to make it a personal priority to do our best in avoiding being a victim and prisoner to those "urges" that we limit our journey with.

You intimately know most of your often addictive habits. They're the same urges that seduce us time and again, guiding us to think and act in ways that have only brought us suffering in the past. They beckon us back to unhealthy ways of functioning, habitual thought processes that reek of distraction and pain, and ways of thinking and being that limit us in the expression of our truth.

We're all challenged to listen for and embrace better approaches to life—approaches that are on our side, the ones that help us refine ourselves towards our truth and guide us toward creating peace.

So listen, listen quietly for that sweet whisper from within, the one that points at a place that you only know through your heart.

"It matters not how you connect with the silence, as long as you do!"
-Mark Stearn

There are potentials for wellbeing that allude us; a sense of ease and peace that we simply miss because of our preoccupation with how we perceive our problems. We get stuck in unproductive, pointless thinking about difficulties that often are really quite meaningless or trivial—more engrossed with what we think is our struggle than what's, in truth, most important in this life.

So often, we're stuck feeling attached to what we think is "the" issue, chewing on it, contemplating it over and over again in our heads, and in our distraction, we miss the opportunity to be alive in our life. We forget that we're here to see our life with a fresh and different eye, seeing it gentler and with more clarity. We're here to grasp the opportunity to experience life with a greater sense of wellbeing and peace. Basically, to live our life in a more authentic way that's closer to our heart. So, go ahead and drop all that head spaghetti. It's only getting in the way of you being alive to life.

There's a point in life when we're all confronted with the naked fact that our emotional wellbeing is our most vital commodity and it requires and deserves our consistent and loving attention.

We're in charge of doing our work to enhance the state of mind we walk through life with, and when we really, really "get it," when we realize that our state of mind has a direct impact on all other aspects of our being, it helps us put our life in line with what's important. We realize, without question, that the body does, indeed, follow the mind.

So we have great incentive to work on the health of our thinking, to attend to our mind. If we want a healthier body then we need to step up our game! We're ultimately in charge. Be the influence that inspires your own personal higher state of wellbeing. Be careful with your thoughts. Our bodies are like puppy dogs, they'll follow your mind everywhere.

One of the many tricks we need to learn in life is how to entertain a thought only as long as that thought needs to be entertained. There is a planned obsolescence built into every thought, a higher quality of existence for it to evolve to, and allowing it to live longer than it's intended leaves us stuck in the thought and steals us away from being present in our lives. In releasing our attachments to our thinking, we allow fresh thought to evolve.

Sometimes you just need to step back and reclaim yourself!
Enough said.

RECOGNIZING THE
gifts IN THE *wound*

THE LESSONS OF BEING HUMAN

"Character cannot be developed in ease and quiet. Only through experience of trial and suffering can the soul be strengthened, vision cleared, ambition inspired, and success achieved."
-Helen Keller

What is there in life that we can't learn from? What's presented to us that isn't chock-full of experience—dramatic, exciting, mundane, funny, and sad life experience? What works and happenings of this life don't hold unseen messages and lessons of the heart? What of this world isn't able to unfold with a little wisdom for us?

Let yourself consider that every event, all the many situations of life are potentials for growth; that they're lessons that help us meet who and what we are. That all our life challenges and considerations come with a form of guidance that assists us in understanding the world a little better—to better grasp the deeper purpose of our presence in it. This is where our experiences, whether good or bad, hold the keys to learning about life. Life is meant to be infinite in its structure, to have many gifts behind every experience, even the moments that hurt. Even our deepest wounds hold gifts. Often, the largest, most important gifts of growth and wisdom learned come from our wounds. It's never a question of whether the gifts are there, only if we can open enough to explore them and all that life holds for us.

"With everything that has happened to you, you can either feel sorry for yourself or treat what has happened as a gift. Everything is either an opportunity to grow or an obstacle to keep you from growing. You get to choose."
-Wayne W. Dyer

    Stuck in contemplation and frozen in our anxious thoughts, our inflexibility and our attachment to fear and worry, the chatter of the mind can become so deafening, so loud and distracting that we can hardly recognize the whispers of our own heart. Even when we're aware, our attempts to quell the internal chaos and disruption, to listen to what's most precious within, can feel like an impossible chore. But life is as it is, and it has a way of continuously begging us to persist, to hold strong in our listening, coercing us through all of its shenanigans to pay attention to our core, to be present to our gift, and to remember that there are diamonds in that-there heart, making all our attempts at listening worthy of our struggle. There are always diamonds at the end of the line when it comes to the heart, always precious jewels that come forward when we learn to listen to what lays within, and all we need to do is remember how to listen, to open to the whisper that is, indeed, what we are.

    Our intention of giving voice to and speaking from our heart is perhaps our greatest challenge. Every time we do it, every time we succeed in communicating through the core of what we are, we tend to evolve ourselves a little, as though we're catching up with our own soul. But pray you never catch it, for it's in the hunt that we define the passion of our search, and it's here where we continuously refine the understanding of our own heart—a journey that can only endlessly expand within you.

Our illness, our pain, our emotional turmoil and our human struggle is never exactly what it appears to be, it can never be what it was meant to be when we're stuck in suffering about it. Difficulty naturally comes to us in this life. It's part of the makeup of being here and being human. This world seems designed to cultivate struggle, creating some quality of heartbreak in our lives that makes our human condition feel more vulnerable and pushes us towards living in a state of distracted thinking and subsequent dysfunction. And if we don't keep an eye on the quality of our thinking, we end up buying into the suffering of life and never really approaching the lessons, the gold held in the difficulty of it. Life always requires us to see our pain differently from our suffering in order for us to move forward. We're asked to embrace our vulnerability and struggle as a gift that allows us to feel our very human emotions rather than fearfully avoiding them, missing the life in the lessons because of our resistance to the struggle associated with it.

Living through the heart simply requires us to endure and open to the vulnerability of our pain. The quality and frequency of that pain is a variable depending on the situation and the quality of thinking we use in negotiating through it. But if we're human, we will feel physical, emotional, and even spiritual pain in this life, and we experience it at the levels that we do because of the fact and gift that we are, indeed, human. We've been endowed with capacities of love in all its forms, including grief, sorrow, sadness, disappointment, and frustration, just to name a few, all because we've agreed on a higher level within ourselves to use this life to move forward and grow. Growth comes with struggle and discomfort, but it also comes with the added benefit of bringing us the motivations that help us find our truth and know ourselves.

When we resist our pain, when we try to repress our feelings and our human capacities for emotion, we inevitably shift ourselves toward fear. We end up stuck in our distracted behavior and thinking, and ultimately suffering far beyond the lessons of our pain. We no longer function as we were meant to in the processing of our lives and we stop moving from our core. We may move forward in life, but we rarely grow forward until we acknowledge and heal our wounds as best we can. Accepting that life can be hard and painful, and that some wounds are bound to require more work than others, but that in our desire to live fully despite our tendency to know and get anchored in that pain, needs to rule the day. This acknowledgement was well expressed by Peter O'Toole in *Lawrence of Arabia* when he said, "The trick is not minding that it hurts."

At best, living life in an extended state of fear, stuck in the fight or flight mechanism, is a misuse of our DNA. At worst, the willing participation is in a conspiracy where society wants us to believe that everything is always a problem, and staying fearful is necessary in a world that's just inherently untrustworthy and unsafe.

But we're here to figure out how to live outside the fight or flight paradigm, to help create a gentler internal world for ourselves, while at the same time playing our part in creating a gentler external world.

> *"If we can stay awake when our lives are changing, secrets will be revealed to us—secrets about ourselves, about the nature of life, and about the eternal source of happiness and peace that is always available, always renewable, already within us."*
> –Elizabeth Lesser

Our existence is a symbiotic relationship between hearts.

The world awaits your shift, and it uses everything and everyone to continuously push you in every possible way so that you can partake fully in its gift.

The gift of reclaiming who you are.

You mean, on a higher level of consciousness, we're all actually choosing to play roles for one another to support the communal journey we're all on? Yeah, okay, it's a funny way to think about life, and a bit unorthodox, but when you look at life from the perspective of spirit trying to guide us through our journey, it's easy to get the impression that we're all participating in one another's life with deep underlying purpose. That we're all here, moment to moment, working on ourselves and simultaneously sacrificing for each other on a higher level. We may not always get what's going on in any particular moment, but when we can let go of our need to understand exactly what's happening, it allows us to see that this sacrificing for the bigger-ness of the journey happens between all of us, all the time.

Our pain and growth, in ways, seem to be bonded together. The caveat to that is suffering or apathy. They tend to internally magnify the issue at hand or disrupt the lessons offered. But when you observe all of us from a spiritual distance, it becomes clear that we help one another into or out of the lessons of life, regardless of the pain, and even though we may never be aware of our spiritual agreement to do so.

So step back and take a look at where and how our lives unfold through one another. There are no mistakes, even when you think there are. The truth is, we just can't do this journey alone. We must agree to help and interact with one another. When you take a closer look, you get a good sense of what you've had the opportunity to become through your life. A little observation on your part reveals the lessons and evolution that wouldn't have been possible otherwise. You simply wouldn't be you without your perfectly evolving, though often crazy, life. And this is true for everyone else involved as well.

So, no matter the circumstance, everybody is constantly given the opportunity to grow. It's a fact. No matter what, there's always opportunity for everyone to become more than what they were, to understand life on higher level. This happens on a level which exists beyond the mind. It's from a place where we've agreed to teach one another how to be in this world with spirit—at least that's the goal. It's an "I teach you, you teach me," environment we've been born into. A symbiotic relationship between hearts.

When we can look beyond the ego and the drama that we think is happening to us and open to the lesson that seeks our heart, huge benefits can open up in our lives. We become a deeper version of what we're meant to be in the first place. So keep yourself open to the bigness of this journey—a journey you were perfectly designed to participate in, along with everyone else.

A final note: On a human level, we're not going to go up to everyone, give them a great big bear hug and say, "Hey, thanks for sac-

rificing yourself for my journey! And I was happy to be there for yours as well!" If we did, for sure, somebody would be trying to throw us into the loony bin. But on a spiritual level, you can honor everyone for their sacrifice, and you might even want to say, "Thank you, and I wish you well," at least from your heart.

The bottom line is that we all agreed to be part of an infinite world where we could interact with each other in infinite ways in order to evolve in ways that go far beyond simply being alive. We're here to evolve together as spirits in human form, and when we're done in this world, we take the essence of our life and what it's been with us.

So honestly, don't sweat the details, someone's getting something out of your pain!

Things go wrong. Yup, that's just part of life. You're either resisting it or open to approaching the "what is" that's in front of you. The quality of thought you interact with this "what is" with is going to define how you live with it. Like Eckhart Tolle said, *"What could be more irrational than resisting what already is?"* It can seem like an awful big challenge in this human world of ours, but we're here to figure out how to deal with whatever's going on in our world and learn how to let it move through us, not get stuck in us.

Our lessons of anxiety, fear, and the difficulties of life create the fertilizer that we can use to grow with. It prepares our hearts to cultivate a courage meant to blossom within and through us.

> *"We must learn to regard people less in light of what they do or omit to do, and more in the light of what they suffer."*
> *-Dietrich Bonhoeffer*

Never let your past struggles and difficulties define who you are in the present, ever! When you do, it's only because you've allowed it. When we live through our past mistakes, dramas, or even successes, we've chosen to restrict ourselves to the limitations of that memory, define ourselves in a way that limits our growth forward. But we can always choose differently when it comes to our thinking. We never have to let our past dictate what we choose as our future, it only limits us, restricts our journey to where we've already been rather than where we can go and might very well love to go.

Memories hold potential for us. They hold lessons we can benefit from, and they help us retain the emotions that remind us that we're human, and together, we know the joy and the struggle in life. If we can learn and remember who we are without getting wrapped up in our old pain, we can use our memories for the greater benefit of our journey. We need to be discerning with the memories we entertain. We have to allow them to unfold through us in a forgiving, compassionate, and understanding way, to come forward in a way that helps us cultivate truth and self knowledge, a way that helps us become a part of the greater good in this world. So embrace whatever gift is held in a memory. It may not require holding onto it very long. As a matter of fact, learning how to let it go might be the very best way to embrace it.

Use your life and all the good and bad things that happen in it to cultivate compassion for others.

Often, the most difficult events in our lives provide the greatest potential for our personal growth. They present an opportunity for us to cultivate understanding and grace for ourselves and compassion for others. As we heal from our own pain, we naturally assume a role where we can relate better to the struggles and experience of others. We find that place within ourselves where we can identify with the pain, anguish, and confusion we all feel. We get, from a heart level, that we have all felt the same struggle. This is where we become observing students of life, using the very heart of who we are, connected to the hearts of others.

This process of knowing others through knowing our own pain encourages us to not take our bad times so personally. When we see our lives with grace, we can see how our difficulties might add to our lives when we don't let them own us. Here, we can experience the events of our lives in a more communally human way. We can approach one another in a more matter-of-fact way, because we're all human, we all struggle with he same kind of problems. We're all in the same humanity boat, and there's no surprise when we find others struggling in life—we realize that we all come here with similar challenges. This brings with it an ability to use our life as a learning tool, to see its good and bad moments as lessons given to us to help us cultivate deeper compassion and greater understanding for our journey. It's through this kind of understanding of our life that we can find a way to better nurture the gift of life. It helps us see a gift beyond our pain and wish the same for others.

We are truly all the same.

So caught up in concern about myself, I forget that you, too, have struggled in relationships and in life. I forget that you, too, have had pain and betrayal, and within that lapse, I have forgotten to be patient and loving. In allowing myself to remember that we are the same, that we all struggle, I open my heart to yours and, in that, I pray we both can find space to heal.

As long as we stay anxiously attached to our experience as a *problem*, solutions have no space to present themselves.

When we're looking for solutions to difficult issues, it's easy to think that anguish is the only language we know to navigate those waters. This is not true. There's always a better way than sitting in our suffering, we just have to get out of our own way and set the challenge off to the side. There's an unknown better way yet to be discovered, and setting things aside gives wisdom a chance to whisper its curious solution.

"The trick is not minding that it hurts."
Life is painful in its very conception.

From the beginning to the end, we are destined to experience emotional pain, physical pain, and pain of a spiritual nature. But if we only ruminate on the pain of life, we lose touch with the beauty that abounds and surrounds us. We end up only experiencing that which we insist on thinking about—our pain.

Through the act of not clinging to our pain, we open a door that inherently invites something more to come through us. We invite freedom, we invite ourselves to live life from a place of wellbeing that reflects our deeper truth, a truth stronger than fear.

Who am I and who do I become in the absence of my suffering, free of my pain, my anguish, and any of the emotions that I've defined myself through in the past? When I walk forward in that light, who am I? What does that person look like? The one who's free from the opinions of others, free from defining themselves by anything but their heart, their divine brilliance. What does that look like? How does that feel? And who do I become then?

"The truth is that our finest moments are most likely to occur when we are feeling deeply uncomfortable, unhappy, or unfulfilled. For it is only in such moments, propelled by our discomfort, that we are likely to step out of the ruts and start searching for different ways or truer answers."
-M. Scott Peck

Pain is not the enemy. Pain is simply your body, mind, and spirit asking for help, seeking to find balance, peace, and opening to deeper healing.

"The best way to get rid of the pain is to feel the pain. And when you feel the pain and go beyond it, you'll see there's a very intense love that is wanting to awaken itself."
-Deepak Chopra

In our recognition of being off the path, we can be brought to our knees, made to see our world from a different perspective. And from this place on the ground, perhaps for just one beautiful moment, we become humbled, freed from our desire to judge everything and everyone, and we become alive in that more prayerful place where we all don't look so threatening and unforgivable.

Sitting quietly, the mind tends to move into and explore our memories. They might be happy, playful memories that cultivate gratitude and feelings of having been blessed, but we also tend to move toward our old pain, ruminating over our difficult times, our memories of the suffering of life that seemingly left us dumbstruck and lacking any movement forward, absent of any movement toward love.

We can all can get stuck in a variety of stagnated thought. Stuck in believing that others are unforgivable for how they may have hurt us, or that we're unworthy of love ourselves. We sit there, living in our past, chewing on dead situations, holding and fermenting our anger, our resentment and fear. And we stay stuck in those addictive negative patterns, we believe in them, we believe they'll somehow sustain us, when, in truth, they only sustain us in fear. And in that place, we receive nothing but that. We end up holding our fear, bitterness, and resentment close, believing that's what we are, that's what's important, and all we really ever accomplish is a slow death inside ourselves.

We know that nothing is more painful than losing our way, nothing. Why would we choose to live here? Is there any good in this? Perhaps we think we're protecting ourselves by maintaining ourselves

in fear, trying to create some safety and control in our vulnerable world. And yet our spiraling fear is what keeps us in our misery in the first place. It's the mouse trap of the soul and the bait is the illusion of control, power, and safety, created through the many faces of fear we so readily and habitually attach to and believe in.

Life requires our personal leap of courage to move beyond fear. It's a required curriculum for this life. Subsequently our real work on this journey is one of believing in something more than our fear, it's one of embracing and embodying something better, something that reflects the strong and beautiful quality of love, no matter the circumstances. This is our journey.

> The cloud of suffering is but a lie that distracts us from our truth in an attempt to keep the perception of darkness versus light alive. What would we do if we knew there was nothing but light?

Every shadow requires a source of light for its creation.

The Lotus Flower

We originate in and operate from a formless flow of infinite energy. Wisdom and truth naturally unfold in and through us endlessly towards love, but like the lotus flower, we do require a little mud to help us grow.

*"Some people grumble that roses have thorns;
I am grateful that thorns have roses."
-Alphonse Karr*

*"Life doesn't give you the people you want. It gives you
the people you need: to love you, to hate you, to make you,
to break you, and to make you the person you were meant to be."*
−Walt Whitman

JOURNEY PROMPT

Has there ever been a time in your life when you've looked around at all the people walking this earth and simply felt compassion for everyone's pain, difficulty, and anguish brought forward by this human condition that we all struggle to negotiate through?

No matter what, when you come home, you're visited by ghosts you thought you grew past or left behind. They spring forward to renew themselves and re-establish the process of growth that you have been either avoiding or unable to see because of your absence. Welcome them. They offer a road to freedom, bumpy as it may be.

JOURNEY PROMPT

Next time you visit a place where you grew up, or any place where you experienced important and difficult parts of your life, even contacting a relative, sibling, or friend associated with those times, pay attention to any of the old thoughts or feelings that come forward—good, bad, or otherwise. Now, they could be things that you feel you've already dealt with, or they might be memories that haunt you daily. They can even include joyful times and memories, because sometimes we get so caught up in how good things were *back then* that it steals our attention and we forget to be present now.

The point is to pay attention to the charge that we hold onto that is associated with the past, and to open ourselves up to seeing it differently. After you've found your attachment to a limiting memory, ask for the wisdom to see it in a fresh way, ask to see it in a way that serves your highest good and the good of others, and then set your thoughts to the side, understanding that new thinking will naturally present itself, and all you need to do is come back and be in your life now.

There will be times in all of our lives where we just need to step back and allow our world to be what it is. To gratefully say, "Thank you," to everyone who plays a role in our world. It doesn't matter what they did, what pain they've caused, or what disruption they've brought into our life—we just need to step back with gratitude and say, "Thank you for playing a part in this journey toward freedom." And from there, we step forward, through the disruption and back into our world, dealing with what needs to be taken care of and, most importantly, never forgetting who we are.

> "Between stimulus and response there is a space. In that space is our power to choose our response. In our response lies our growth and our freedom."
> -Viktor E. Frankl

JOURNEY PROMPT

In looking past all the craziness of life, can we still remember who we are? That's where you contact the living warrior within you, the essence of strength and courage inside your being who has the gall to say, *"Enough! I'm done with this quality of life. I will not do that, I do not do that anymore! It's time to move forward toward what feeds me, what feeds my heart!"* Your life warrior is the one who can take part in and be present in this world in a full way without losing themselves in it.

Okay, this might seem a bit cliché, but think about it: *there's no such thing as failure, just fresh opportunity.* Understanding the word "failure" without attaching judgment to it and making it into something bad or creating a permanency around it is, perhaps, the most important part of understanding the art of succeeding.

JOURNEY PROMPT

Do you remember learning to read in elementary school? I do. I was always in the super-duper slow readers class that couldn't have their milk break (I'm aging myself) because we weren't done reading *Run Dog Run* (still my favorite book of all time). And my entire day was made up of failure! Except on the playground, when they relented and let me out. But what I'm saying is that it was all part of my process towards me, towards success as success was meant for Brian Roscoe. I kept on going with reading and English, even though I detested it, struggling with it through my entire education! But success found me through, and because of all my failures, I also found success.

It's your failures that have always brought you your success. Hold both gently.

"I've missed more than 9,000 shots in my career. I've lost almost 300 games. Twenty-six times, I've been trusted to take the game-winning shot and missed. I've failed over and over and over again in my life. And that is why I succeed."
–Michael Jordan

There is a lot of freedom you can claim in understanding that the only one responsible for you is you.

Sometimes, we can get caught in a more frightful world of our own construction; a place in our heads where we can't seem to see past ourselves and our pain. And here's the kicker: you made it, and you can unmake it!

At different times, we all get caught up in the struggles of this broader world and our personal world. The problem might begin as an event outside of us or an event in our lives, but it ends up living, growing, and evolving in our heads, taking up excessive mental real estate and coloring our world and our hearts, all because our emotional reality became deeply rooted in an outside experience rather than through a quality of thought directed by our heart. Yes, we get held captive in our heads by the stories we get stuck in. This can prevent us from seeing all the different sides of an event and knowing a more complete truth around it. It's our ability to step back and allow our thinking to loosen up and unwind a little that naturally opens us to the best solutions to any problem, all without losing ourselves in the process.

JOURNEY PROMPT

When we're stuck in our thinking, stuck embracing all the stories of struggle in our head, it's not always easy to acknowledge that we're the ones doing that—we're the assemblers of the story and creators of our own stickiness... ummm... state of being or feeling stuck. We really want to find something or someone else to carry the load, but the truth of it is that we're experiencing life as a drama of our own construction, creating a world where we can't see past ourselves or our pain, and it would serve us well to move past those disruptive habits of the mind.

The most loving thing for us to do here may simply be to admit our involvement to ourselves, to own it and step forward into our life as we gently try to understand where we just went and how we got so caught up in our story. Understanding the very human trait of getting stuck in a story opens us to the potential to shift away from it and move back to experiencing our lives in a fuller way rather than through those potent and pesky lies of the mind.

This beautiful life we live is not always so easy, and sooner than later, we're bound to get hurt in the body, mind, or in our spirit. It's certainly not the fun part of being human, but getting hurt is a real and authentic part. Our hearts are made to be broken and, sure enough, in many ways, we get hurt. Behind every wound there lays a gift, a wisdom, a lesson, a strength.

Look for the gifts that exist in the wounds of life. They're often hidden, but always present, and we just need to open up to them and be willing to explore their secret message.

JOURNEY PROMPT

Our wounds are painful, and we don't like to revisit them if we can avoid it, but when it seems impossible for us to let them go, it helps to know that their gifts will be presented when we are ready to see and understand them.

Our growth is a process from within, requiring only a willingness to open up to our healing. It may be slow going and we may become impatient with the journey, but the other option is to remain blind to our hearts and to live in our suffering, and when you're stuck in that suffering, it's refreshing to know that you can always choose again.

I'm less tolerant of the pain I still have.

Years ago, I was working with a patient who had chronic back pain. After a while, she seemed to be getting quite better. Later in her care, when I asked again about her progress, her comment was, *"I definitely have a lot less pain, but I feel less tolerant of the pain I still have."* She begrudgingly, yet patiently, understood her process, and was willing to see it in a truthful way that she was doing well but still had work and healing left to do.

Our struggles, bad habits of the mind, and emotional pain work the same way. We get impatient with ourselves, seeing our slow spiritual and emotional progress with frustration. Even when we're making good progress, we're still so intolerant with what does show up.

Here's where we need to recognize the truth of the situation:

As we do our life-work, navigating our emotional and spiritual struggles, we evolve. The challenges have shifted, they may be handled better than they used to be, and the negative thinking, though still there, is now less frequent, has shorter visits, and is less intense than it was. It doesn't often seem like it in the moment because we're less tolerant of the pain we still have, but that's still progress, and we need to own it!

So, we continue to walk forward patiently while allowing the depleting qualities of negative thought and behavior dissipate and settle away. And we persist in our often rocky journey of learning love.

JOURNEY PROMPT

Think of any situation from the past that may have emotionally blown you away and left you miserable and upset. In the past, it would have created a far bigger struggle in your journey than it does now. The same thing can occur today and you don't take it so personally, or get nearly as uptight about it. It just doesn't hit you as hard as it used to. Well, we call that wonderful progress! See it as forward movement and give yourself kudos for your work. You're doing a little better because now you know a little better. That's perfect. Now, keep moving! There's always more road to be walked.

> "And the world cannot be discovered by a journey of miles, no matter how long, but only by a spiritual journey, a journey of one inch, very arduous and humbling and joyful, by which we arrive at the ground at our own feet, and learn to be at home."
> —Wendell Berry

Sometimes you just need to step back and reclaim yourself!

Life can hit us hard sometimes, and after things settle and we're sitting there, in our stunned silence, we wake up a little, we raise our eyes up from our problem and realize that we got lost, that we misplaced a certain fire, a spice of life, the zest of remembering that we are love. Stuck in that old place of forgetting ourselves, our strength, wisdom, and deeper connection to our truth, begs us to reclaim ourselves, and to move back into our light.

The irony to this slippage is that without it, without that dichotomy, without the polarity of slipping away and pulling yourself back through the sheer force of your willpower and spiritual courage, there is no journey.

So, be grateful for your imperfections because they are the perfect hands helping you to redirect in a deeper way, guiding you to pull back towards yourself and your truth. The deeper and more personal the snag feels, the deeper the reward.

JOURNEY PROMPT

When it comes to connecting with your truth, recalibrate, recalibrate, recalibrate, and don't stop. It's an endless process. We can never reinforce ourselves back towards our journey too many times. As a matter of fact, the journey requires it! So, heads up, this marvelous machine of yours always needs oiling and a little more tweaking. It's all about the maintenance, which is an endless process.

Sometimes we just need to step back to ask, "What the hell is this?"

    Some part of our journey we're not yet familiar with begins when we hold up our heart to God and ask with an irritated tone in our voice or with outright anger, "What the hell is this? What is this guiding light? What message lives here? You need to clue me in, buster! Because no matter what I do, this thing will not shut up! And all it can say, over and over and over again, is how would you like your life to unfold now? And the only answer I have is to surrender into what flows through me in each miraculous moment! And then I hear the calm and confident whisper, 'It's all just part of the journey.'" And then I don't know whether to be pissed off or take a breath. Usually, I take a breath.

JOURNEY PROMPT

I can get pretty frustrated with life, feeling like I'm on a treadmill that keeps me moving forward, going nowhere. It's not necessarily true, but that feeling pushes me—it leads me to a place of questioning how I'm living my life and if re-evaluation or change is necessary. So, I ask: **am I willing to do this work at the expense of living my life?**

    And then something happens, like I find a quote from someone who has probably asked that same question.

> *"Do you have the courage, do you have the courage to bring forth this work? The treasures that are hidden inside you are hoping you will say yes."*
> *-Jack Gilbert*

    And I have my answer, because my heart speaks to me.

The struggles and challenges we encounter in relationships are very often our best training in forgiveness, remembering love's presence, and stepping into our lives with honor. And, after all, isn't that ultimately what we've all come here to learn?

JOURNEY PROMPT

Often, we need to prep our wounds so our healthiest healing can occur, so they don't just turn into scars that inflict what feels like more needless pain. But the truth is, this is how life unfolds, this is how we move forward, this is how our earthly experience is. We get hurt, are wounded, and we're meant to heal. The process doesn't happen to be fun, it can and usually does hurt, but the lessons are exactly what we need, and often prolific. And it's all about the lessons.

Regret. Ah, yes, sweet regret. It can own us. And when you think about it, it kind of disrespects life without meaning to, it might even be a misguided way to try and reclaim something that was never meant to be. And it's yet another way to express our disappointment at not being perfect. Living in regret is a way of saying that we don't trust in the depth and purpose of our life. That what has unfolded for us was a mistake. Regret indicates that we walk around feeling less than, that our life is somehow wrong.

But regret is really a misconception, misdirected thought, because it questions the truth of what is now. We imprison ourselves in the spiraling void of questioning the perfect unfolding of our life. And most importantly, regret overshadows and potentially eliminates our connection with gratitude. It blocks our ability to live gratefully with what we've been given.

Regret is an example of misplaced values and misplaced trust in the sanctity of life; not trusting in the essence of life, and paying attention to something else far less important than the precious gift of being.

JOURNEY PROMPT

Can you see any situations in your life where regret has overpowered your mojo, your zest for living? Where it's left you feeling less than and unhappy with your life?

In the absence of regret, what would life have looked like for you? How might you have spent your time differently? Could you have, would you have, approached life with more vitality?

If so, think about what that would look like, consider who you would have become in that moment.

If not, why? What holds you so firmly that moving forward into being more alive to life is impossible?

Loss is never easy, but we're offered growth and freedom through loss that we would not and could not have chosen on our own. Perhaps it comes through an agreement made through our more spirited connection—one that our minds were incapable of understanding the consequences and value of. Regardless of its origin, we need to ask ourselves: how can I best embrace this change?

> *"What could be more futile, more insane, than to create inner resistance to something that already is?"*
> -Eckhart Tolle

JOURNEY PROMPT

It's easy to find ourselves stuck in our pain, our negativity, our judgment, our anguish. All these thoughts and feelings are meant to be teachers, red lights on the dash of a car, put there to let you know something's not working right in the core of who you are. They don't represent the main plot of your movie, they simply represent the tiny sub-stories meant to make the reader, you, question the story at hand, and then hopefully feed you back toward the main plot. Our disruptive thinking was never meant as anything more than a wrinkle in that fabric, a thorn on the rose, a simple glitch meant to remind you to question who you are so that you can readjust yourself, and hopefully, as quickly as possible, point yourself back to the life you're really meant to pay attention to. So don't get too caught up in the difficulties of life, they're put there to challenge you to remember what's important. While they're doing their thing, don't give them too much of your life, but just what they need to help make you a

better person.

Periodically, we're all re-visited by the mental burdens and ghosts of our past challenges and struggles. Although these challenges never die, they do tend to morph a little to give us opportunities to heal in a deeper way. These are the difficulties that we thought we'd matured through, grown past, and left behind, but like most things in life, there's a lingering effect—an effect that's hard to see or that hasn't yet presented itself. And as with anything that relates to our evolution in this journey, there's always more work to be done, additional healing, deeper lessons to learn from our challenges.

So life springs forward to challenge us again, to help us renew and re-establish that part of the journey that still holds a charge, still has a lesson it wishes to teach that we just hadn't seen before. We might greet it with compassion or be shocked or surprised it came up again because we've either been avoiding it, distracted by other interests, or it just wasn't time to do the work for that part of the problem just yet. Either way, it's just another opportunity to learn about yourself.

JOURNEY PROMPT

My friend, Angie, was struggling to feel like she was enough. She had slipped back into an old belief system that began to grow and expand in her mind, until she caught it. Angie recognized that belief system for what it was and allowed it to reset into something kinder and more productive. Ultimately, Angie realized that it was time to imagine a better way, to believe something new.

So while in this atmosphere of her personal growth, we met for coffee and I asked her, as usual, what was new, and she said with a smile, "Oh, there's lots of 'new' happening today." Curious, I rephrased my question, "So Angie, what's the 'new?'" Her answer was profound, self empowering, and it put a smile on my face. She said, "The 'new' is the truth, and the truth is love. The truth is that I am enough." I smiled and thought to myself, "Well, that about says it all, Angie, for everyone."

Moral of the story: The bottom line is that you are love, and in that, always enough, so no matter what's in front of you, always seek the truth beyond the shadowy stories that can get created in the mind, because that's where we find our freedom.

We find our truest healing when it's filtered through the pathways of the heart. No matter the struggle, the issue or problem, unless we open our healing up to the heart, unless we walk through the doorways that we hold within our hearts, we can never fully embrace our healing or our pain, and we can never move beyond it.

Ask yourself: What wound, what difficulty, what struggle exists in our world that doesn't require the heart for us to move through it with grace? When is the heart not required to heal and forgive?

When struggle and difficulty is held in the mind and kept from moving through the heart, when we insist on intellectualizing and figuring our stuff out rather than feeling our way through it, our journey becomes an aspect of ego, opening us to fear, possibly judgment and even arrogance. But when understanding comes from the heart, it's real, it's authentically us, and its healing stays alive within us. We meet every day with a wisdom that supersedes the mind, and we greet every remembered moment, difficult or not, with more love.

Yes, there are doors that exist in the heart—doors that are ours to open, that we have to walk through, that we can't claim to know the other side of until we look deeply into our pain and our struggle. It's here, in the emotional heart, that we find our opportunity to open and pass through doors that open to our growth and our healing. We can't see beyond our pain when these doors of unexplored feelings are locked closed. Our journey is to cultivate courage, the courage to open the doors that scare us most, to choose to brave a journey through which we might just be able to find a deeper part of ourselves and rediscover our truth.

JOURNEY PROMPT

In opening up and walking through our doors, the life experiences that expose our vulnerability, we open a gift, we uncover our spirited strength, touching a quality of wisdom in our hearts previously unrecognized. This is what we're meant to do, what's important in life, the reclaiming of our truth, of ourselves, our lives, freeing us to become more complete, more human.

So when you find yourself working through a life issue, whether it be old or new, find some space within yourself and ask: What's the strength, the wisdom lesson locked behind this vulnerable feeling? What door within me do I need to open so that I can heal?

Because behind every wound is a gift—not a gift we have to contrive or create, but a gift that we simply have to be willing to open up to.

Over time, it becomes obvious to us that our loyalty to our desires and to our ego makes life difficult, and it's in our connection to the heart that we find our antidote.

No one comes into our lives without reason. Lessons in love, forgiveness, judgment, friendship, and compassion all come with the gift of great opportunity to help us step forward. with big steps or little steps—we are here to facilitate one another's path. The predicaments we find ourselves in are not so important. What's important is how we address them and the quality of heart that we bring to the moment.

EXPANDING
perspectives
OF THE HEART

"So divinely is the world organized that every one of us, in our place and time, is in balance with everything else."
-Johann Wolfgang von Goethe

In our spirited communication, we speak ever so gently through the heart, and we expand together. We also expand alone, in our prayer, meditation, our quiet moments, listening to that whisper within that tells us what we're meant to be. All this has the power to bring us into new perspectives to walk through life with, like journeying hand-in-hand with a friend, a partner who understands the truth of us—the truth that we are all hearts, all inspired to be the love we were created in.

Given the opportunity to complain, most people will… but you're never forced into it. It's a choice.

At the end of the line, what have you given the final say in your life to? There's a definite struggle between tapping into the truth available through our free will and the yearning of the heart, versus relying on the values, judgments, and addictive habits of society, culture, friends and family. The ideas present to our minds as possible ways to "live life right." So, at the end of our line, do we stick to the dictates and habits of the mind, the qualities of right and wrong that our need for acceptance pulls us toward? Do we hold to the ideas of others that define how well we've done and whether we're enough? Or do we rely on our heart and the free will thought derived through our own understanding of what brings meaning in life?

It's in the birth of our thinking where we first choose our life and its direction, and its in giving our minds back to that life and exchanging our dreams and our illusions of self-concept for the whispers of the heart that we re-enter our life. Here, we allow our first death to move through us as we give up our dreams. This is where we find ourselves, define our higher truth. This is our place of remembering.

We can go back, listen to the old dogma, the fear, our own "logic," but it's the whispers radiating from our heart that meet our true need. It's those whispers, no matter how difficult they might be to hear, that hold our truth and our desire. Use those to color your world, use that to guide your life. Soon enough, you will see we're only meant to follow our heart as we walk forward in this world. No one can do it for us, no one can show us exactly what that looks like. It's through our own volition that we keep walking forward, walking past the many deaths of our fears, and always opening more into an aliveness that feeds the heart.

"It is what it is." A phrase we all commonly use that has a duel application in life. It can be used as a phrase to give us permission to give up, to be resentful, negative, or lazy about an issue and avoid being in our lives, or as a tool that recognizes what lays in front of us without the fear, judgment, and underlying frustrations attached. "It is what it is," used as a Power Statement, helps us approach what is now with an access to a wisdom that lends us the opportunity to open to new thought without the old strings of tension attached. "It is what it is" helps us step back and say to ourselves, "Now let's approach it from this new space, a place of simply seeing what life is presenting now. Let's open to the creative flow that's within us from the point of what is, rather than living life through resisting what is." Truly, it simplifies and strengthens our lives, allowing us to expand rather than contract into the world.

"There are only two ways to live your life. One is as though nothing is a miracle. The other is as though everything is a miracle."
-Albert Einstein

Bliss comes from giving up expectations, releasing the need to know the future of you, how you fit in this world. Bliss comes from giving up the need to control all the outcome of things and simply allowing the now of life to unfold as it was meant to be. This act of allowing comes through our no-judgment mind, giving up the need to know why things happen the way they do, not in questioning our breath, but in allowing the gift of life to be present within every breath.

Our memories are the perfect little ways to remind us of our lessons. Using them to define the quality of our lives is way overrated and darn close to completely unproductive in the scheme of life. So be grateful for your memories, even the unpleasant ones. They're simply bookmarks in life, not the book.

What's the difference between self-love and self-improvement?

They're exactly the same,
because if it's not love, it's not improvement.

If you continue to follow your old ways, you simply end up in old places. That's just the way it is. It's important to always give yourself permission to choose new, to begin again and open to the possibilities that previously didn't seem like a viable option. A simple shift in perception can make all the difference in how you walk forward.

Our journey is not about if we live, that's already been decided, but how and when we choose to live it for ourselves.

When we finally become aware of the blatant fact that this world is ours to experience, ours to live in as much or as little as we desire, to approach in a way only we have control over, we're then confronted with a choice. The choice is not if we walk forward, or if we do, in fact, live our lives, but when and how will we do our living. And we're asked to choose the quality of thought that we want to enter our journey with, knowing that it's that choice which will most define our experience. Our participation in this world either inspires our heart or depletes us, and there's always one question for us to answer for ourselves: are we rejecting life or welcoming ourselves to it?

Diamonds at the end of the line.

Sometimes we don't grasp that what we're given in this world is absolutely perfect for us. We try to organize things so that we get what we think we need, or what we're persuaded that we want through the media and society's values, but in truth, it's what we're given that holds the most meaningful charge. That's where the diamond is.

I had a vision in which all the potential people who could be in my life were lined up from most desirable to least. The first vision was organized through my ego and what I thought the line should look like. At the beginning ten percent, I saw a friend from the past that I thought fit well into my categories of appropriate. Near the end, another friend that I thought was not exactly right for my life. This was my ego creating an order to the line that it deemed appropriate.

Then I asked what love and universal intelligence would desire. The one at the front of the line disappeared and the friend near the back moved right up near the front of the line. When I saw this in my mind, I was shocked at the clarity of the message. There are always diamonds at the end of the line when the line is dictated through the ego. If we knew all that we're missing by not trusting what lays beyond our desires, we might give up a little of that ego of ours.

I'm in awe of the choices I make versus the choices divinely inspired for me. After my diamond vision, I was stuck with questions: How can I have chosen so wrong? How could I've been so wrong? How could

I have allowed myself to go down a road that had so little promise. But the truth is, there is no wrong. We just need to be willing to admit that to ourselves so we can grow past it when the time is right.

> *"In the light of trust, as it develops slowly over time, you will find that you are a privileged child of the universe, entirely safe, entirely supported, entirely loved."*
> –Deepak Chopra

We know we're distracted from our true nature and disconnected from ourselves when we think that we're the ones in charge of how things will work out in the world. We tend to personalize things to the point that our desire to have things our way becomes our primary concern in life; that we can micromanage and control our world and the world around us to make sure that we are comfortable. But this need to micromanage our lives and create the illusion that we have control only reflects the difference between being in your head or living through your heart. As we've said before, we're either stuck in our heads or alive and present in our life. That doesn't mean you don't put effort into life. To the contrary, you will absolutely have many concerns you need to act on. You just don't let outcomes and expectations own you, you do what's necessary in the situation without attaching to it at the expense of being in your life.

There's a lot of personal power to be gained by simply letting go of outcomes. And like the Buddhists say, release yourself from the I, me, and mine's of life.

JOURNEY PROMPT

What quality of life micromanagement do you need to let go of so that you can move forward and breathe deeper in this world? So that you can free yourself or others from your tyranny, even though you have it worked out so your control comes across as nice. You know what I'm talking about!

1.

2.

As we work our way through life, our minds try to entertain and comprehend either the limitations or opportunities of love. With the perception of limitations, we shut ourselves down and deny our truth. But even with the most difficult to embrace opportunities of love, we open to huge potentials of what we can be, because it's in our hearts that we open to truth—infinite truth within.

JOURNEY PROMPT
Choose any situation, struggle, or challenge. Ask yourself:

Who are you and who do you become when you open to all that love is?

Who are you when you close yourself to what love can bring?

There's a concept often taught that we should reach out and grab life, and that's a really wonderful thing to do. But in letting go enough, letting go rather than chasing or grasping, you give life the opportunity to embrace you in unimaginable ways. It helps you open to a presence in the world rather than a drive. When you can release yourself enough from your ideas about what you want and how things need to be, well, that's where you really open yourself up to living—living in each moment rather than the future, living through trust rather than having to make the next thing happen. Life just flows through you without the limitations of the habits that come from a controlling mind.

It's when we think about the future that we can't see the perfect moments now. Life is simply a series of perfect moments, one after another, and it's in our fear that we make them unavailable to us. The truth is, right now is always perfect. It doesn't mean that you don't have things to do, that nothing's going wrong, or that you don't have things you want to do later, but right now, this moment, this breath, it doesn't need anything. It's just a perfect moment, worthy of your presence in it.

This is part of the journey: Finding that place within yourself where you understand that things are perfect just as they are. That doesn't mean we don't need to work on stuff, trust life, do what has to be done, but when it comes to your ideas about how everything should look and be, let go of all you're expected and forced outcomes and realize that everything is perfect just as it is, even as you're washing the dishes or disciplining the kids. It's all just life unfolding, no matter what or how we label it.

JOURNEY PROMPT

Allowing ourselves to be taken by what life brings forward challenges us to let go of our expectations and judgments about one another as well as what a particular situation "should" look like. In letting life grab us, we open up to allowing everything to be what it is. Thus, the phrases, "It is what it is," or, "Everything's just as it's meant to be."

Most of our human problems aren't solved by relentlessly trying to think them through. We solve them when we give ourselves permission to let the solution find us. So, look beyond the words churning through your head and listen for the quiet answer; the whispered solution.

JOURNEY PROMPT

It seems like we can sit with our friends or by ourselves for hours trying to figure something out. We spend our days trying to understand particular circumstances in life, grinding our teeth and tensing our shoulders as we try to take control of our lives. But it's the very act of letting go that often proves the most productive in our journey. You have to let go of your issues, your problems, your struggles, because if you don't, it's not you holding them, it's them holding you. And they will never release the answers to you. It would kill them.

When we do our work to cultivate a higher state of consciousness for ourselves, it naturally draws out the same from others, and perhaps they'll develop a desire to discover their very own flavor of peace as well. It's a fact that we naturally touch others when we do our work, and then it's up to them to keep that train on its tracks and to do their own.

JOURNEY PROMPT

We touch one another on this journey, and within that, there's an influence. This influence can go in any direction. When we are inspired, we can inspire the people around us. When we're crabby, we can give others permission to be negative. We can make judgment and prejudice seem almost normal when we participate in it, and then others see it as acceptable. This happens politically as well as socially, and it's our job to create something better. It's always our job to expand into life through the heart.

Like Marianne Williamson says, shine! That's what we're meant to do. That's our journey. To do anything less is to deny our inheritance, and to turn away from our authentic truth.

> "As we let our light shine, we unconsciously give other people permission to do the same. As we are liberated from our own fear, our presence actually liberates others."
> -Marianne Williamson

One of the most dangerous things we can say to ourselves regarding our emotional wellbeing is, "Finally! I'm all done working on myself!"

JOURNEY PROMPT

In my younger years, as I fought through the lessons that came with my life, I remember saying to myself, "Finally! I'm all done working on that!" At the time, I thought I had made some progress in some aspect of my life, but I was also smart enough to know better. So, I usually ended up saying to myself, *"Uh oh, I just challenged the universe to bring on the next step in my growth! Uh oh!"* And sure enough, inevitably, another lesson, begging for work, appeared down life's road. And of course it did, because that road never ends!

When we shift our thinking a bit to take away some of our desire to be rich or famous or admired, our lives open up to a multitude of previously unexplored possibilities, which we are then free to explore with heart.

This is true of many habits of the mind, and often, our biggest challenge is to first recognize the disruptive quality that any particular desire has on our psyche before we can open up to what life might be like in its absence.

JOURNEY PROMPT

You've got to learn to let go before you can play catch with life! When it comes to our desires, weaknesses, issues of any kind, it's helpful to acknowledge them and then imagine, with a strength, what life would be like in the absence of that quality. What would it look like, how would it feel, and who would you be—what would your life become in the absence of that?

It's from here that we begin again. Always time for a fresh start!

"Whatever you feel, you become. It is your responsibility."
-Osho

How often do we get caught up in a story about our lives that we feel the need to believe in a particular way? Seeing it only from one perspective at the expense of paying attention to the truth, and even our happiness? And in this story about ourselves, do we open up enough to ask the important questions of life, like: Am I seeing this properly? Does it really matter if my story is true or false when all it does is keep me in misery and anxiety? Our stories don't have to define us. You can choose fresh with how you choose to look at anything, and if you do choose new, choose a story you can live with, breathe with, a story you can find some happiness with.

JOURNEY PROMPT

Re-structure an old story stuck in the mind—a life situation, drama, circumstance that you've held onto in a particular way for a long time that you'd like to put a different twist on, heal it somehow.

Re-structuring a story:
We feel challenged to change the charge of a story or a memory when it occurs to us that the story or incident we're holding onto is not serving us anymore. It creates too much pain or internal disruption for us to continue live with. The reasons nay be as numerous as the stories, but the bottom line is we just need to re-define it for ourselves, we need to see it differently for the sake of our wellbeing.

The objective is to identify a memory we're holding onto emo-

tionally and look it over. It might help to answer some questions like: How are you holding this story now? What kind of a charge does it create in your heart? How important is your particular attachment to that story? Are you willing, and would it serve you on a higher level, to see it differently? Can you make it a part of your life journey to somehow heal or forgive the pain that surrounds it?

Suggested steps:
Define the story and the quality of emotion that you've accumulated around it, look at how it exists within you. How are you holding onto that memory? When it comes up, what happens, where do you go?

Step toward your story as an observer rather than a participant, as though you were a scientist watching an experiment from afar and taking notes. Spend a moment feeling what being in that memory is like for you, take note of it, and then step back away from your experiment knowing there's healing to be done.

Until you can see where you are, it's difficult to figure out where you want to go.

Once you've figured out where you are, all the emotions, the pain, the betrayal, all of the ideas and thoughts you're hanging onto around that story—ideas and thoughts that do nothing for you now but maintain you in a place that's kind of stagnating to the heart—can be released. Your ideas around your story may have some truth to them, you might have the best of reasons to hold onto them, but if they're creating misery rather than growth in your life, why would you want to?

It's just found its time; time to see the story with different eyes, find more compassion, more human understanding, perhaps even more forgiveness through it.

Put all the participants in your story in a big room. As you observe them, remember they are just like you in all ways. They just want love, they make mistakes, there are many things they just don't understand about life yet, they have difficult upbringings, ones you don't understand, they have lots of unresolved pain, and they don't feel safe forgiving one another much less themselves.

Understand that there's a precious gift behind every story that creates pain, we just have to be open to seeing it, understanding how it makes us more human, identifies our vulnerability and thus our heart.

Know that you're not being asked to forgive the bad deed, you're simply being asked to not identify another through their deeds. You're being asked to see them as "people in pain asking for help," as not so different from yourself.

Open yourself to the idea that no matter what your story tells you now, you can always find a new way to look at it, always find a fresh, gentler approach within and for yourself. That approach can touch others, and that's wonderful, but it's really for you. It's really your gift to you.

Precious Choices

Sometimes you just can't get to where you need to go until you walk away from where you're at. It doesn't mean the change is easy. It's not likely to be painless, and it may not even be remotely pleasant. Leaving something behind may not make your life easier at all. As a matter of fact, you might feel thrown on your ass and confused afterwards. So it's important to hold your choice high, because there's life in that choice. Your truth exists in choosing what's most important, in questioning the most precious use of your time and your life, and when you realize that you're sacrificing your heart and soul from where you are standing, choosing anew means choosing life.

JOURNEY PROMPT
Taking it a little further, walking a little farther.
It's life, it happens. We get to the point where we can clearly see that we're going to get what we get as long as we stay where we're at. We don't really know anything past that, because what's in front of us is simply new, and we have to approach it, open to its freshness, knowing that moving forward could absolutely take a couple tries before things settle.

These are our "precious choices," which are often difficult to make because we have to choose between the way we used to do things and the way we now have to do life. But they're choices that we've been brought to because, at our core, we're required to always reclaim our heart and soul in this life, to live through our truth. Can we really live any other way?

"Abundance is not something we acquire. It is something we tune into."
–Wayne W. Dyer

Be responsible to the story of your life. You may have absolutely nothing to do with why things have happened in a particular way around you, but it makes up the first half of your story, and the way you respond to it makes up the other half. That's your responsibility; that's what you own.

The good news is, once you realize that you own your responses, life presents you your choice!

The bad news is, once you realize that you own your responses, life presents you your choice!

See, it all depends on how you look at it. I prefer the good news! But either way, we are asked to move forward from within when we choose to own our life and how we participate in it.

JOURNEY PROMPT
Homework
This is really a question of blame. We might be able to blame something or someone for an event that happened, but we can never blame them for our response to that event, especially after the initial reaction. That's your freebie. After that first reaction, the second thought always belongs completely to us. That's our responsibility.

Have you ever responded poorly to something and found yourself trying to make someone else responsible for the way you participated (i.e. "I acted this way because you did that."), do you remember how it felt? Do you remember how uncomfortable your own behavior made you feel about yourself, how awkward that was as you were trying to pull it off?

What did you do?
Did you walk away?
Did you admit what you were doing to anybody?
Did you end up apologizing?
Did you apologize to yourself?
Did you own the story that you tried to create as you tried to rationalize to yourself what actually happened?

"Each man is questioned by life; and he can only answer to life by answering for his own life; to life he can only respond by being responsible."
-Viktor E. Frankl

We all have ideas about who we are, concepts about ourselves and our particular personality types that we incorporate into our interactions with others. We might bring out different qualities of ourselves depending on a particular social situation. So we hold onto our box of tricks, our ideas about ourselves and our familiar behaviors that we attach ourselves to. There's a wide range of possibilities, from self-concepts that we think make us humorous, strong, smart, to those of being weak, timid, anxious or less than, and we incorporate those traits as part of our personality. We create a belief system that perpetuates our behavior.

But we need to step back and see that some of the ideas and behaviors we've attached to are simply engaged so we can effectively integrate or survive integration with one another in this world. It's an impressive moment when we can stop for a second, take a breath, and question the productivity of how we're relating to the world; ask ourselves, "How authentic is this to who I am? And is there a more precious way for me to relate to my environment?" Basically we're asking, "How can I better relate to my world with love, with a heart that truly reflects my authentic truth?" This step into yourself isn't always easy. It requires opening to previously unexplored inspiration, it takes charisma and spunk to accomplish, a real zest for growth.

So, I came up with this…

Careful now! If you didn't believe that you thrived so much on (name your positive or negative trait, behavior, habit or addiction), you might find yourself looking in the mirror and seeing a reflection that's even more amazing than the one you thought you knew.

JOURNEY PROMPT

Make a list of some of the different qualities, attitudes, habits that you might use as you relate to others. It doesn't matter if they're positive or negative, or if you don't even have a category for them, just explore some of the ways that you integrate yourself into this social world, or out of it. What do you do to habitually shift in order to feel protected or funny or in control?

Examples:
- You go into anxiety and find a reason walk away.
- You become a class clown and feel compelled to make people laugh, even in serious situations.
- You use your acquired "driving skills" as a way to release your frustration, anger, anxiety, and emotional resistance toward life and change.
- You try to take control of any conversation because you're uncomfortable with feeling like you're not being seen or included in life.
- You say nothing in a conversation, even though you might even like to contribute and have plenty to say.

Keep in mind: This exercise is simply an exploration who we are, it doesn't mean you have to change anything. The point is to help you pay attention to who you are. Making sure that nothing is in our way of being able to walk through this world free from anxiety and fear, self-contrived or otherwise. Wherever we can illuminate fear-based behavior, we allow an opening to a more authentic way of living. We create an opportunity to open ourselves to the world.

Focus. Focus. Focus.

I often find myself asking patients if they want to be healthier in five years than they are now. "In all possible ways?" I add. Inevitably, their answer is an enthusiastic, *"Yes!"* and I follow through by telling them, "Then you have to think like it, act like it, believe in yourself and live like it, starting now. You can't start in five years." This is a powerful concept to adopt for anyone who wants to fully embrace the best of what life can offer, and what they can offer life.

Live life as though you want everything money can't buy! Continuously encourage all the *something more* you can imagine—more healing, more love, a deep and great appreciation for being alive. This means paying attention to the quality and consistency of your diet, your exercise, and the tone of your thinking. When you pay attention to how you live, the quality of your life takes care of itself.

JOURNEY PROMPT

Healthy and new ways of being need to be chipped away at. It doesn't happen all at once. You don't just turn around and have it dropped in your lap. It's work and it requires your participation. And you can't start in five years if you expect to be there in five years, you must begin the process now, even if it's just planning your strategy, you have to start somewhere and then chip away as though you're creating the sculpture.

Create a list. Explore the ways about yourself you'd like to change in a span of time. Say, five years. Make a spirited list, a physical list, an emotional list. Explore all the ways that you would like to recreate and renew your world. What obstacles would you like to overcome? What strengths would you like to cultivate? How would the heart of you like to change things up so that the truth of you can more easily unfold to this world?

1.

2.

3.

What are my biggest obstacles to my truth, my health?

Having answered this, what would it feel like to walk that new walk?

"Success" as a State of Wellbeing

I think we all already inherently know this. We all know that real success, the success which flows in and through us, is not simply derived through the accumulation of things or the amount of money we make. It's not attained by our ability to produce perfect grades in school or generate exceptional work performance reviews. Success is not anything that's born from the material fruits of our labors. Those things are nice, but they have no bearing on our personal success as human beings. They don't really influence the quality of who we are as much as the quality of who we are influences them. Material success is only a reflection of what society says is important, but most of us know better than that.

A successful life comes from the opposite direction. It's our personal feelings of a very heart-centered success that drives the deepest purposes of our activity.

True success as a human being is quite free from the constraints of society. It's the kind of success that has a longevity and grit to it, a strength that emanates through us, a willingness to shift and change in its ideas and concepts. True success doesn't require anything to be derived from our outside experience, but very simply comes from our connection to the gold that we hold within us.

JOURNEY PROMPT

We're created as spirited humans with a built-in neurology, a software, that strives to understand life and grasp the deep definition of purpose that steps beyond the limiting dictates of our ego. Our level of consciousness and the state of wellbeing we're able to cultivate becomes our obvious gauge for success in this world. As thinking beings that think first through our hearts, we're given the opportunity to participate on this planet in abundant ways. We're designed to love and play with each other, argue and fight, to laugh and cry with one another, and explore and communicate about our experience as the spirit-fed beings of light that we are.

So, as best as you can, be present to the experiences of living, find the joy in your life, open up and let your heart enter the room first, and let it be your guide forward. There's way too much great stuff going on here, in this inspired life, to look the other way just because you're uncomfortable or scared. As a friend of mine says, "Human up and be alive to the ride!"

Sometimes I find myself being in my world, stuck in judgment. I create and hold on to opinions about people I don't even know—smokers, people who look or act different from what I'm comfortable or familiar with, people who (in my opinion) obviously aren't taking care of their bodies, who behave in ways I consider inappropriate, (fill in the judgmental thought on all of the above).

So, I ask myself: What would it look like if judgment was absent from my mind? What would it look like and who would I be without my judgment dragging down my thoughts and my heart?

JOURNEY PROMPT

Sometimes it's more important to ask yourself as you're judging another person or situation, not who that person is, but who does your judgment turn you into? Is that really how you want to spend your time here? Does it work to anybody's advantage for you to hold on to opinions that don't really feed the world or human condition in any worthwhile way? It's important to pay attention to and explore what you become in all situations, to acknowledge who you are when you can let go of your judgment and walk forward with a bit more acceptance and mind that actively wants for a life that's more loving. So, just remember, it's all just part of the journey and all you're in control of is the attitude you walk into the room with!

The fact that you have the capacity to recognize your faults is basically a miracle of self-awareness in itself. Consider yourself blessed simply in having the ability to see your own mess, the ability to avoid getting caught up in everyone else's stuff and simply owning what is yours. What a beautiful step forward in the story of you knowing you!

JOURNEY PROMPT
This may have been best said by Albert Ellis in his quote below:

"The best years of your life are the ones in which you decide your problems are your own. You do not blame them on your mother, the ecology, or the president. You realize that you control your own destiny."
-Albert Ellis

In our desire to expand beyond our self-imposed boundaries, step past the fear-based limitations we've created for ourselves, it's necessary to look at everything that keeps us from fully being and living. It's what's required of us so that we can walk forward in life, remembering who we are and how we're meant to live in this vast world. We have to stay open to all the tools available to us, especially those that make the best mirrors through which we can look deeply into ourselves and be inspired to grow.

If you've substituted the world's riches for the richness of an open heart, there's still time to recalibrate!

JOURNEY PROMPT

It's never too late to begin again, and often, it's preferable. When you recognize that you've gone in a direction that's just not productive, it's not getting you where you want to go and you don't like where your life is headed, well, begin again. Begin again at whatever level, in whatever way you need. Just pick a piece of life and start refinishing it! It doesn't have to be a big piece. It can be small—some way of thinking that you've grown past and you want to find a better approach to. Refinish enough different parts of your life and, before you know it, you've created a whole new world for yourself.

Be alive to yourself inside life's most important questions.

Okay, now you might be saying to yourself right now, "Just what the hell does that mean?" And I've got to tell you… I don't know, but it sounded good. I got nothin' more.

But in my creative imagination, I think we have to be alive to ourselves in order to connect to that huge place within that guides us toward our self. We all have questions we're trying to find answers to, questions about who we are and how to live in this world. And it takes the deepest kind of connection within, an understanding and uncompromised link to our wisdom, to find and know peace amongst all the pain and difficulty of life. Perhaps that's how we live, by adhering to and living by our natural wisdom, embracing that place where we both fully experience and step beyond our own human frailty.

And isn't that the point of our humanness. Because we'll always get pulled into pain, and part of the the journey is to finally get to the understanding that it's just another temporary moment, and it always shifts. How it shifts depends on how we see our pain and the quality of our attachment to it. And how can we truly know any of this unless we stay alive and awake to the questions of life?

Lovingly, the universe will gladly find a way to make you feel uncomfortable, out of your element, itchy in that skin you finally think fits so well. After all, the universe is infinite in its wisdom and pointed in its lessons, and you, you are its very special project! Why would the universe hold back when it knows you have so much potential?

> "Our loved ones will continue to press every button we have, until we realize what it is we don't want to know about ourselves."
> –Byron Katie

Our feelings of safety come from being able to accurately discern the difference between a true threat and a thought that mimics a threat. They are both thoughts, but only one is based in truth, and often the only real difference between an authentic and an imagined threat lays in your quality of thought about it.

Learn to be entertained by yourself—let yourself laugh at your mistakes, try and find the humor in all the antics and self-induced pranks that got you into whatever funky place you happen to find yourself at in life. Be okay with your own naiveté, and be willing to see your psychological innocence. We all make mistakes until we figure out a better way. Let yourself recognize that all the craziness and all the drama is part of the journey of being human, part of our human path back toward peace.

So laugh at the shenanigans that come with being human, because, trust me, getting stuck in the witch hunt of self-criticism is a real drag. Laughing, finding humor, not taking life so personally is way better and brings way more love, healing of our hearts, and it makes life a lot more fun! It's a win-win! Or, as a young lady once told me, "We get more happy-action that way!"

**We touch forward into life with all of our choices,
and all our choices touch all of life.**

Our lives and our choices are far bigger than we imagine them to be. We touch the world in good and bad ways that spark a quality of life that influences future generations. Whether we want to believe it or not, we touch future generations in infinite ways we can't begin to imagine.

Have we lived our lives accordingly? Are we now living our life as though a future matters? Do we behave as though our touch forward has profound meaning to future generations? Can we see that what we do now brings deep meaning to the very core of the journey we live now, and touches the journey of others?

The Great Law of the Iroquois held that tribe members needed to think seven generations ahead (about 140 years) in determining how the decisions they made would benefit their children in the future.

We're all asked to be conscious of our choices, to create a life based in truth. There's no limit to how we can love our world, and no end to the ways we can destroy it—our physical world as well as our internal state. Daily, we're presented with the physical, emotional, and spiritual choices of life, challenged to create good, even at our own sacrifice, or perpetuate that which is of no real value.

Personally, as I get older, my purpose is more clear. Should I die, the world moves forward, not much changes and everyone will continue

on their way. But my moral role of patriarch, mentor, or just healthy old guy leaves me with the question: **how can I live my life right now, so that as the world moves forward, I have left it in a better way?** I do what I can so that this question can guide me in all my life choices.

Of course, this doesn't require me to produce anything except a life based in truth. There is no limitation to how we can love this world, and, inversely, there is no end to the ways that we can destroy it. So we find ourselves continuously presented with physical, emotional, and spiritual choices: **create something good, possibly at our own sacrifice, or perpetuate that which is of no real value and wait to die.**

I often need to remind myself to reset and deepen my standpoint towards gentleness and love. It's a place, an internal destination, that I find I have to continually refocus on, because as I get caught up in my life I tend to forget what's important.

As we progress through our journey, we naturally experience higher and lower states of wellbeing. The ups and downs can feel disconcerting, especially when we've experienced a new higher level of wellbeing, and then slipped back into old lower patterns. The distance can feel overwhelming and our sudden downward slip is frustrating and can be downright scary to us. We thought we had conquered that place, made so much wonderful progress, but there it is again, the threatening and bleak feelings of our old ways.

However, this is not the truth of it. Our perceived setback is not what it seems. We're not slipping back to where we were. The old ways are simply whispering at us, and the contrast between light and dark seems more extreme because we've expanded the distance between them. We might be tempted to react franticly, believing that we've lost ground, but its more like walking between a dark room and a sunny patio, we have to let our eyes adjust to the light. When you walk between them, your eyes adjust so you see things with a clarity—sometimes a painful clarity. So as you move through the highs and lows of the journey, take a breath, stop for a minute, and let everything acclimate to the change in your perception of your light.

Be patient with your process, have faith in who you are. It's not that you've slipped away, it's that having spent so much time inspiring yourself, any

little slip into old ways of thinking seems immense. It's a temporary distraction moving through your mind that, in this moment, has caught your attention. You can and will come back to who you are, you'll have even more understanding, clarity and wisdom within, and, in the end, you'll realize you never left.

Sometimes, when we think we're making progress on our journey or that "we've made it, we're all done with *that* part of life, that way of being," we can become arrogant and less tolerant of our slips in life, not to mention the slips of others. We end up blinded from our understanding, kindness, and from compassion itself.

In recognizing that we're intolerant of our own imperfection mode, it helps to take a breath, look back at where we came from and just how stuck we historically were, try to understand that what just happened to us was only a temporary setback, and touch back into our grateful, humble, kind and tolerant state of being. It's here that we remember that there's always plenty of space in this world for improvement, but we don't have to be the example of perfect. We were just immersed in another example of three steps forward and two steps back! It's okay.

JOURNEY PROMPT

Come on, do you honestly believe that you can live your life never looking back at your negative memories? It's not whether or not we look back, it's about where you go with it, how long you stay there, and allowing yourself to gracefully embrace the progress that you have made in life. Otherwise, your intolerance only tempts you to slip back toward old and even worse ways of thinking. It's in finding compassion for the journey that allows us to stay on our path toward something better. So as Tony Horton says, "Do your best, and forget the rest!"

There's a strength that lays in having the ability to recognize the old and the stale ways of life that no longer work for us. They might be tempting to return to, like sweet snacks with no nutritional value, but the bottom line is they just no longer work for us, there's no point in going down that road anymore. It just serves no greater purpose in our lives. And in our strength, we say to ourselves, very simply, "No. I don't do that anymore."

Our old ways are so seductive. It's like they have lives of their own, and they just want to pull us back so they can feel real and in control again. Sometimes you just need to send those characters away with a chocolate shake, thank them for their past presence in your world, and give yourself permission to let them just be another memory.

We all want life to be a great experience, an experience that feels a whole lot better than living in the old patterns of fear we've inherited through the ages and often adopted as our own.

Admitting that and stepping up to its challenge is the first part of our journey toward being there, being ourselves. But first, we have to choose to step toward the healing offered in the challenge of that journey.

No one promised us easy,
but we were promised growth!

Are we such an archaic culture that unless our children, friends, families or acquaintances think exactly as us, hold our belief systems as their own, we're unable to accept who they are, that it's impossible for us to see the beauty of their presence?

How else do we grow but by opening to new thought, by embracing and exploring the flow of different ideas about our world, and by questioning and discussing what can and should be held up as truth, even in our discomfort?

Learn how to pay attention to your mind while communicating with others. We're really not present in a discussion when, in our heads, we're waiting to have our say, eager to let the other know what we know, or prove that we're right about something before we've given ourselves a chance to listen to what someone might have to say. We never give our communication partner the courtesy to talk and be heard. We speak, but have no patience for listening.

JOURNEY PROMPT

Yeah, listening. Really, really listening to one another. This could use a little work from all of us and end up benefiting everyone. Someone once said to me that the most loving thing we can do for one another is to listen, be present with that other person, and process what they're saying—just listen without contriving your confrontational or even helping response in your mind before they're done bearing their heart. All responses will come in good time. Your only job is listening and trying to understand the mind and concerns of the human you're interacting with in the moment. When we can communicate from the heart, and it does take practice, we bring life to the world in a way that speaking through the ego never can.

"When you take the time to actually listen, with humility, to what people have to say, it's amazing what you can learn. Especially if the people who are doing the talking also happen to be children."
–Greg Mortenson

Becoming the matriarch or patriarch of the family first asks us to listen to one another. So, what does listening look like, what does it feel like inside yourself, and who do you become when you're fully present in the listening process, especially with the people you love?

JOURNEY PROMPT

We're all listeners in training, on that long pothole-laden road of learning how to listen to and really hear the heart of one another. It's a process, a lesson, a true journey for everyone. And as we grow in that journey, the quality and essence of our listening grows with us. Patience and compassion, empathy and honoring others' presence takes a seat in our heart when we finally learn to listen to one another. It's an intimate thing, this communication between two souls, and our listening takes on different forms depending on where we are in our journey, but the words we share with one another are big, not just in their concepts, but in the essence of

what communication represents. Speaking and listening at a heart level is literally the flow between two spirits in human form trying to almost prayerfully find common space. It emerges through us, and it holds an almost mystical element to it that we often seem to miss. We often take our communication for granted until we're present to it, into what's really happening. The unification of two hearts. The subjects are often unimportant, but the precious act of speaking and listening is communing with another's soul. It produces some of the most sacred moments in our day. In a very real way, communication is a prayerful interaction with another human. To the mind, it means, "You have my ear," but in the fullness of the heart, true communication is more about, "You have my soul." And on a good day, this is what we evolve into—soul-to-soul communication facilitated through the heart-centered souls that we are while using words, body language, and quiet moments to accent what's really happening. Underneath it all, its simply a prayer that says, "I love you."

So, no matter where we are in our journey, opening to a quality of interaction that goes beyond our words opens us more fully to our spirited human journey. Our responsibility becomes one of listening with a deeper sense of dedication, heart, patience, and wisdom to those we love, and if we've lived life well, we love everyone.

Throughout your day, try and listen more without interruption. Give the spirit opening up in front of you time to express themselves. Try and listen a little beyond the words being spoken and see if something more lays behind them. This is a deeper listening that requires a fuller form of communication that comes through you, and all you have to do is be quiet and listen! What a deal!

In conversation, constantly uttering interruption phrases like, *"I know, but,"* or argument-provoking comments and subject-changing interjections in order to get the "upper hand" in an interaction is simply a disruptor tactic. It's often done because of fear. It's a phrase that takes everyone right out of the miracle of communicating with another being and it kills the potential preciousness that could exist while pulling us away from the present moment. It's an example of a weak form of communication based in fear that distracts us from seeing one another's light because we're so busy interrupting the song of our hearts, the music of communing, connecting with and understanding one another. It totally shuts down even the most basic communication, not to mention the healthy, beautiful, loving stuff.

JOURNEY PROMPT

Choose your communication wisely and without judgment. Learn how to identify when you're not present in communication and find ways to repair that disconnect. Learn how to attach to what's coming toward you rather than your next thought or impending words, what you need to be doing, or what you want to accomplish later. Give your communication partner exactly what you want: loving listening. And then share, together. Because all communication should be honored and viewed as a mystical and miraculous experience, worthy of your full attention.

Live with abandon in this beautiful life and all that it's offering you. Let your essence and your true nature have their way with you as you remember your deepest sense of being alive, self-aware, and infused with the courage found in love. You are an inspired being, capable of infinite expansion, always evolving, always in search of love's meaning, always alive to this life, and in letting your heart take you over, you will only spiral upward. Live with abandon in this beautiful life and you'll find yourself moving into the heart and spirit of who you are and all that you're meant for in this world.

We're taught that most things in life come with a beginning and an end, a success or a failure. So often, we live our life like there's a scarcity or an abundance to our world, and in the strictly physical realm, this may be true. But when it comes to moving through our heart, these rules don't apply. Here, the pure potential for our continuous evolution exists, there are no bounds to it. It lays in our next moment, our next breath. It's in the next lesson, it's found in our struggle and in our joy. The potential for our growth lays behind every door we walk through, and as we enter through them, we manifest a deeper knowing and a more profound understanding of our journey and who we are. Life in all its glory, all its lessons and challenges, is always teaching us who we are, always waiting for our recognition and our remembering of what we're meant to be. So again, I say: Live your life with abandon to all this beauty, all the lessons, the joys and difficulties of being alive that this world is offering you. Embrace this life, your life.

This world was meant for us, created to help us find love, to present us a journey where we can transform ourselves and grow, continu-

ously and without end, until we're ready to leave. In this miracle of living, we learn our truth, how to participate, not in fear, but in a grounded love that supersedes that fear. I won't promise you anything in this world, but I will promise that no matter what you do, if love is attached to it, it will be better and your life will be greater. You will be more of who you are with love. But purpose, passion, joy, these are things you simply need to decide to acquire for yourself, because your choice is life's most vital hope.

"The purpose of life is to live it, to taste experience to the utmost, to reach out eagerly and without fear for newer and richer experience."
-Eleanor Roosevelt

ABOUT THE AUTHOR

Brian Roscoe

DR. ROSCOE specializes in multiple forms of holistic techniques that teach the clients the power behind releasing the emotions that limit life. Through his work on integrating the body, mind, and spirit, Dr. Roscoe helps patients form a deeper understanding of their ability to heal their internal world. He helps them explore some of the many levels of personal growth, while engaging their journey with more meaning, discovering their unique internal wisdom, and restoring a life based in self-love.

DrBrianRoscoe.com
BrianRoscoeAuthor.com

CONTINUE THE JOURNEY

books by Brian

Inspirational Espresso

Get your daily shot of inspiration! In his book, Inspirational Espresso, Dr. Brian Roscoe walks us through the importance of looking inward and questioning ourselves in the interest of cultivating a higher state of wellbeing and, therefore, a richer life experience. With little shots of wisdom guiding you to question your motives, integrity, and direction, Brian helps pave the way for choosing to learn to love better while maintaining a sense of compassion, understanding, and truth towards yourself and all others.

"Our purpose here in this wildly marvelous world is to remember how to expand into a place of deep, multilayered, unconditional love – a love that is, in essence, who we already are and have always been."

Inspirational Espresso will leave hints of truth, inspire moments of wisdom and understanding, as well as mindfully helping us live our lives pointed toward a gentler, more compassionate way while immersed in this fantastic journey of living.

Call of the Heart: Six Secrets to Self-Love

CALL OF THE HEART is the gateway to your journey back to yourself. Roscoe presents a journey guided by love and self-discovery that will change your perspective on life, forgiveness, relationships, and your journey's purpose.

In this book, you will find:

- guidance and inspiration for living through love
- how to discover your inner worth and light
- how to see the gifts in your wounds
- introspective prompts to carry you along the journey
- Listen to the call of your heart, and journey through this book to uncover the six secrets to self-love.

Call of the Heart, Awakened: The Journey of Self-Love

CALL OF THE HEART, in its second installment, takes readers deeply into the journey of self-love. Using all of the insights and tools of the first Call of the Heart book, Awakened steps into the minds and aspirations of everyone who explores its pages, helping them see an enlightened way—the truth within themselves.

In this book, you will find:

- a deep dive into what it means to live with self-love
- how to manifest your inner gifts
- how to elevate your perspective
- introspective prompts to carry you along the journey
- Listen to the call of your heart, and journey more deeply into the remembering of your spirited self.

Power Statement Logbook: Mentoring the Habits of the Heart

THE POWER STATEMENT LOGBOOK is a companion guide to the Call of the Heart series. This workbook empowers readers to take charge of their journey by guiding them through meditations and musings on how to find, harness, and employ your personal power every single day.

In this book, you will find:

- deeper insights into the journey of self-love
- prompts to help stir your inner wanderer
- activities for introspection and growth
- guidance and tips for your journey ahead
- Listen to the call of your heart, and journey more deeply into your personal power.

The New-Now: The Art of Being Right Here, Right Now

We're here to activate a higher consciousness from within to reclaim our own miracle. Our journey was designed to be an inspired one, one we're all meant to embrace, and it's expressed through the gift of a world that infinitely unfolds into each unique life. So welcome. Welcome to your life. Welcome to the journey.

Are you ready to fully engage mindfulness?
Are you ready to honor each and every moment?
Are you ready for a new perspective?

Welcome to the New-Now.

PLEASE LEAVE A REVIEW

Public reviews help independent authors bring you the books you love. If you loved this book, please leave a review on Amazon. You can also leave your feedback on social media by connecting with Brian @drbrianroscoe. Thank you! And enjoy your journey!

www.ingramcontent.com/pod-product-compliance
Lightning Source LLC
Chambersburg PA
CBHW070530010526
44118CB00012B/1090